Girl's Bass Method

Everything a girl needs to know about playing bass!

Tish Ciravolo

Cover model: Sheyna Gee
Interior model: Candace Letterman
Cover photography by Karen Miller.
Interior instructional photos by Larry Lytle.

ISBN 0-7390-3675-0 (Book and CD)

Alfred

Daisy Rock Girl Guitars®

Contents

Introduction

Finally–a bass method for girls!

Two experiences came to mind when I sat down to write this book. The first was when I was a teenager and loved to watch the TV show *Happy Days*. I'll never forget the first episode I saw featuring the character Leather Tuscadero (the younger sister of Fonzie's friend Pinky Tuscadero) playing bass in a band at Arnold's, the local diner. In real life, that was Suzi Quatro–and she was playing a bass! ***Wow!*** I'd never seen anything like that before, and that girl was absolutely the coolest thing I'd ever seen on TV. I was a huge fan of *American Bandstand* and the *Midnight Special*, but had never seen a girl playing bass on those shows. But there was Suzi, pounding and thumping on a bass, and I was totally hooked! Later, I saw the Go-Go's on *Saturday Night Live*. **What?** All girls in a band playing the instruments? I had never seen anything like it.

And that's when I knew I wanted to learn how to play the bass. Today, there are more girls playing bass in bands than ever, but in my estimation, there are never enough. So I hope this book helps you, inspires you, and drives you to be the best female bass player ever. Be a star! Start a band! You can do it, too!

Photo © Neal Preston/CORBIS

Suzi Quatro

For Suzi Quatro, being famous for her leather-clad, tough, wild and streetwise form of rock launched the idea that playing bass in a band was the coolest thing a girl could do. In the 1960s, she started playing in her sister's band, the Pleasure Seekers. By the time "Devil Gate Drive" hit the top of the pops, Suzi Quatro had become a household name.

Dedication

This book is lovingly dedicated to my two girls, Nicole and Sophia; the playful memory of my best friend in high school who taught me how to play guitar, Barbara Haughey; and every girl out there who finds the courage to pick guitar or bass as her instrument. Remember–Girls Rule!

Parts of the Bass

Electric Bass

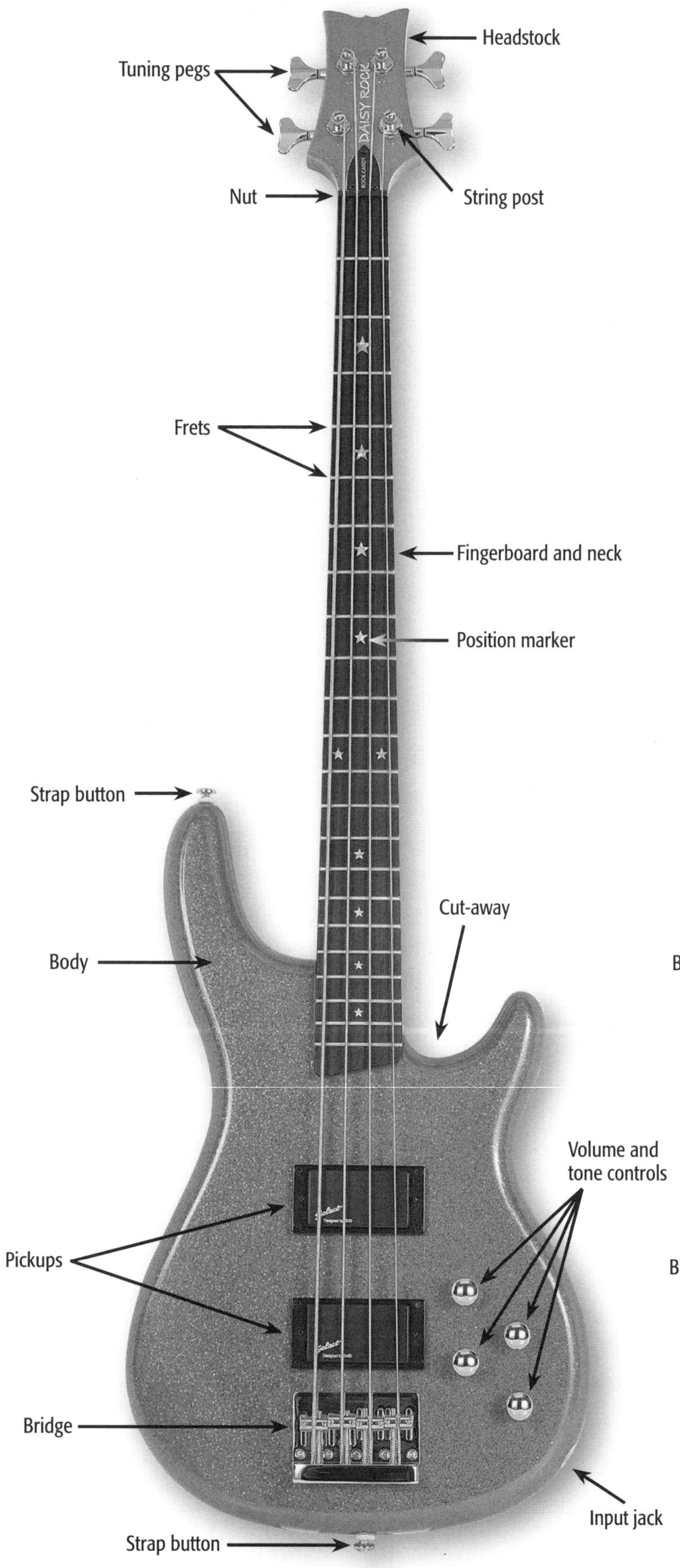

Acoustic Bass

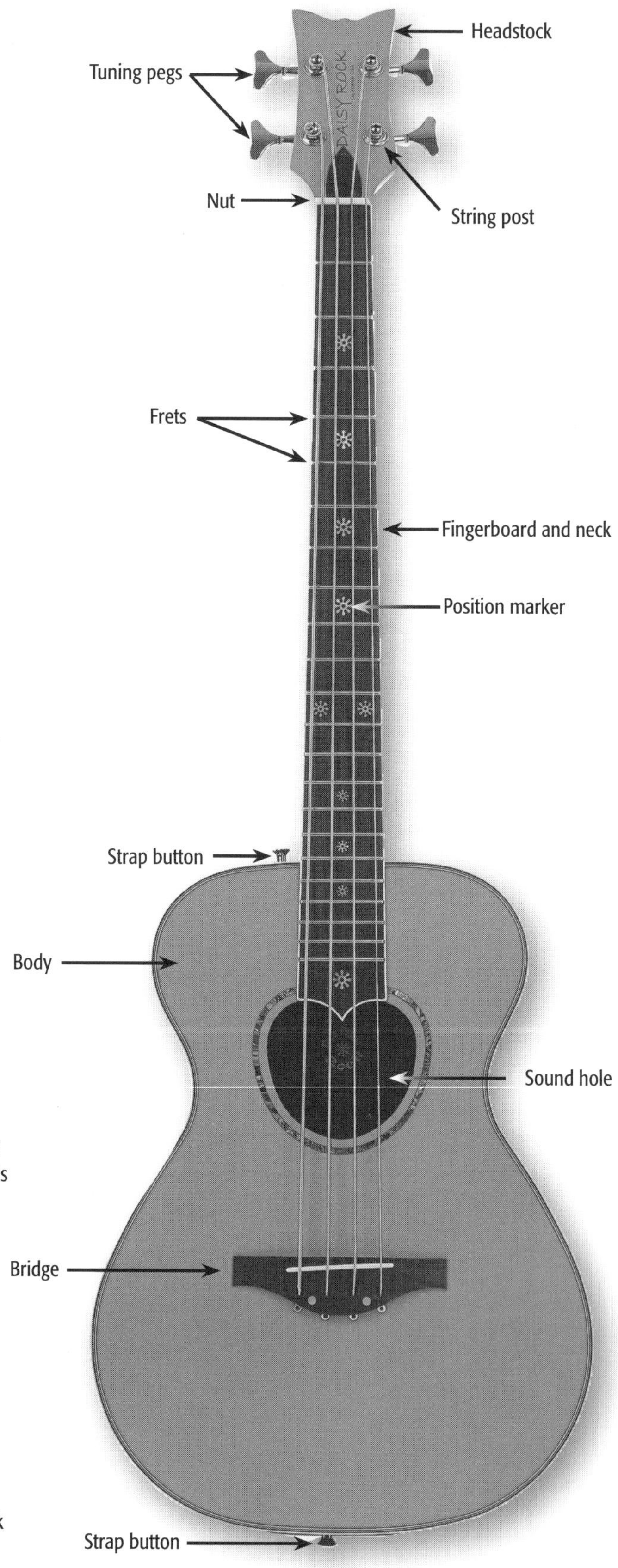

Holding Your Bass

Below are four ways to hold your bass.
Pick the one that is most comfortable for you.

Sitting on the floor.

Standing with strap.

Sitting with legs crossed.

Sitting.

Tuning Your Bass

First, make sure your strings are wound properly around the tuning pegs. They should go from the inside to t he outside as illustrated to the right.

Some basses have all four tuning pegs on the same side of the headstock. If this is the case, make sure all four strings are wound the same way, from the inside out.

Turning a tuning peg clockwise makes the pitch lower. Turning a tuning peg counter-clockwise makes the pitch higher. Be sure not to tune the strings too high because they could break.

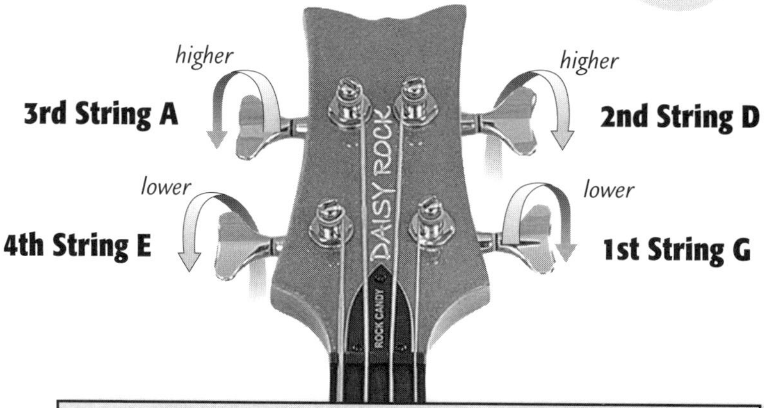

Important:

Always remember that the thinnest, highest-sounding string, the one closest to the floor, is the first string. The thickest, lowest-sounding string, the one closest to the ceiling, is the fourth string. When bass players say "the highest string," they are referring to the highest-sounding string.

Tina Weymouth

Talking Heads, Tom Tom Club

Tina Weymouth's pioneering mixture of funk, alternative and punk rock merged into a new sound that would ultimately land the Talking Heads in the Rock 'n' Roll Hall of Fame. After graduating from the Rhode Island School of Design with no thoughts of having a career in music, she relocated to New York City with some friends who had formed a musical group at college. When they were unsuccessful in finding a bassist who shared their mutual admiration for cult groups such as the Velvet Underground and the Modern Lovers, Tina picked up the bass and joined them. By the early 1980s she was widely considered to be one of the finest bassists in rock, and in 1999 was named on the list of VH1's 100 Greatest Women of Rock.

Photo © Ken Settle

Tuning with the CD

Track 1

Put the CD in your CD player and play Track 1. Listen to the directions and tune each string so that it matches the pitch on the CD.

Tuning to a Piano or Keyboard

From lowest to highest, the bass is tuned to E, A, D, G, corresponding to the keys shown on this diagram. The notes on the bass will sound an octave lower than the notes on the piano.

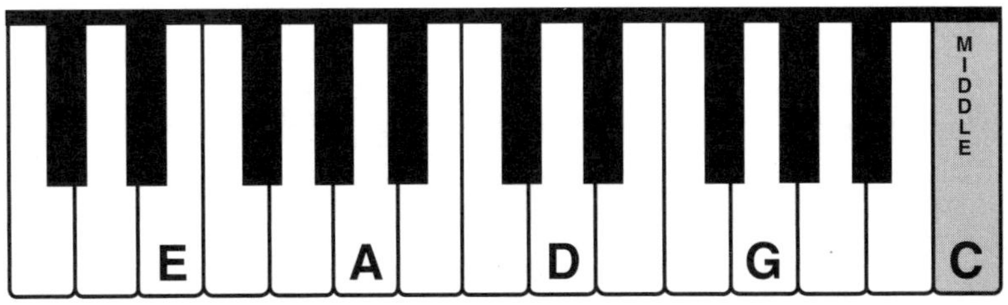

Tuning the Bass to Itself

When your fourth string is in tune, you can tune the rest of the strings using the bass alone. First, tune the fourth string to E on the piano. Then, follow the instructions below to get the bass in tune.

Press 5th fret of 4th string to get pitch of 3rd string (A).
Press 5th fret of 3rd string to get pitch of 2nd string (D).
Press 5th fret of 2nd string to get pitch of 1st string (G).

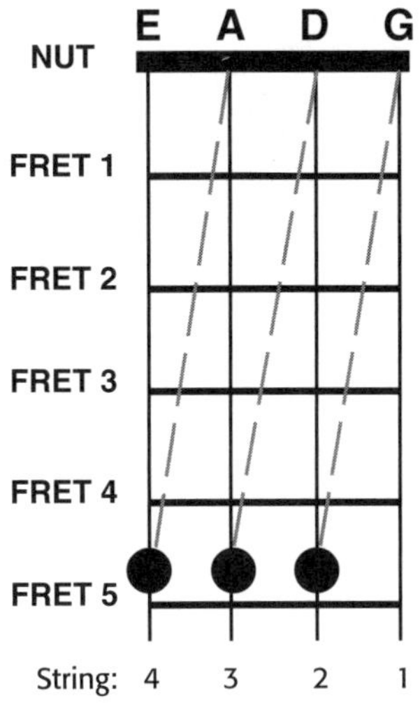

Pitch Pipes and Electronic Tuners

If you don't have a piano available, consider buying an electronic tuner or pitch pipe. There are many types available, and a salesperson at your local music store can help you decide which is best for you.

The Left Hand

Proper Hand Position

Learning to use your left-hand fingers starts with a good hand position. Place your hand so your thumb rests comfortably in the middle of the back of the neck. Position your fingers on the front of the neck as if you are gently squeezing a ball between them and your thumb. Keep your elbow in and your fingers curved.

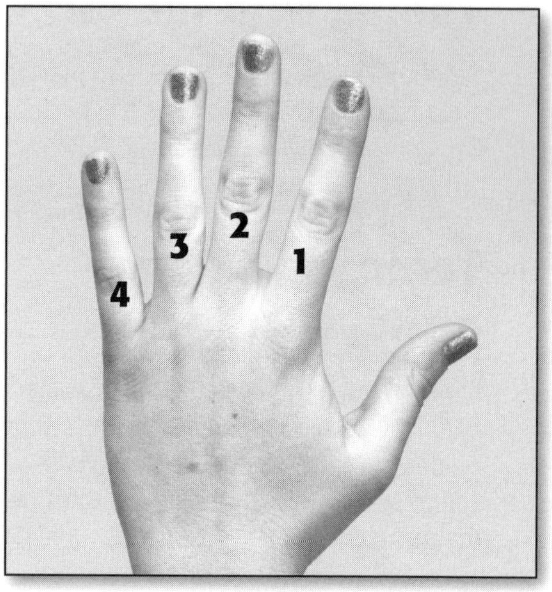

Numbers of the left-hand fingers.

Keep your elbow in and fingers curved.

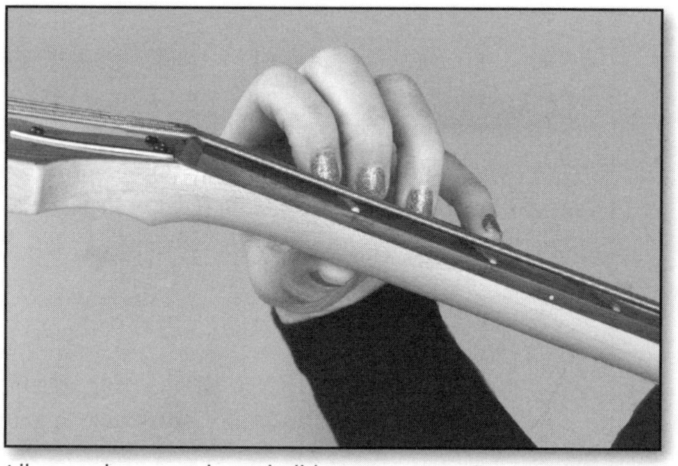

Like gently squeezing a ball between your fingers and thumb.

Placing a Finger on a String

When you press a string with a left-hand finger, make sure you press firmly with the tip of your finger and as close to the fret wire as you can without actually being right on it. Short fingernails are important! This will create a clean tone.

RIGHT
Finger is close to the fret without actually touching it.

WRONG
Finger is too far from fret; sound is buzzy and unclear.

WRONG
Finger is on top of the fret; sound is muffled and unclear.

The Right Hand

Proper Hand Position

There are two common ways of playing the strings. One is with your fingers, and the other is with a pick. Using your fingers may give you more speed and flexibility where playing with a pick will give you a very sharp attack and brighter sound.

Using Your Fingers

Most players alternate their index and middle fingers to pluck the strings. If you aren't comfortable using two fingers, start off using only one finger, and add the other later. When playing with your fingers, it is important to notice that after striking the string, the finger comes to a rest on the next string except when playing the fourth string, where the finger rests on the pickup.

Index finger

In position.

After striking the first string.

To get used to playing with the fingers, play a series of notes on an open string slowly and evenly. Do this with all four open strings.

Middle finger

In position.

After striking the first string.

Using a Pick

Hold the pick between your thumb and index finger. Hold it firmly, but don't squeeze it too hard.

To get used to playing with a pick, play a series of notes on an open string slowly and evenly.
Do this with all four open strings.

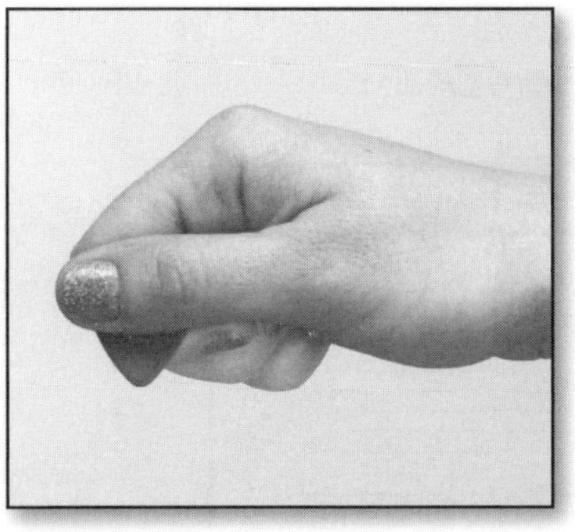

Holding the pick.

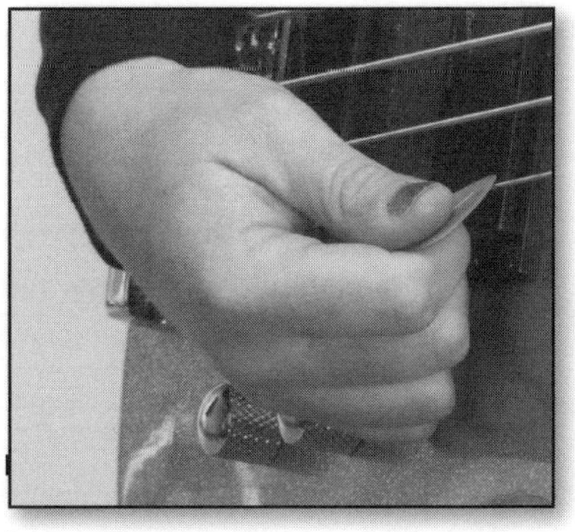

In position.

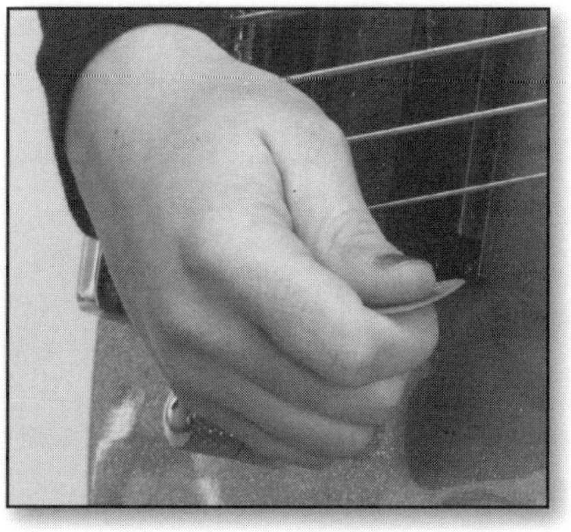

After striking the first string.

The Basics of Reading Music

Musical sounds are indicated by symbols called *notes*.
Their time value is determined by their color (white or black) and by stems or flags attached to the note's head.

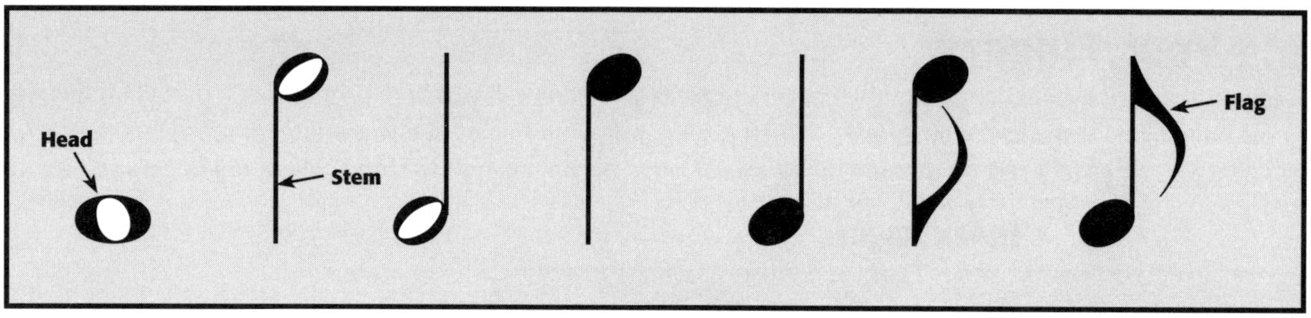

The Staff

The notes are named after the first seven letters of the alphabet (A–G), which are repeated to embrace the entire range of musical sound. The name and pitch of a note are determined by the note's position on five horizontal lines and four spaces between called the *staff*.

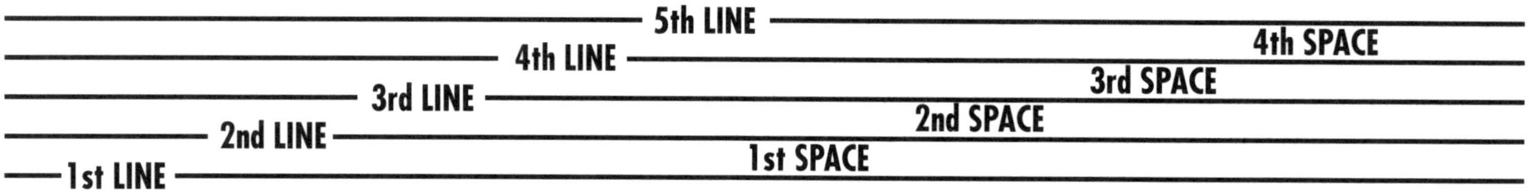

The Bass Clef

During the evolution of music notation, the staff had from 2 to 20 lines, and symbols were invented to locate a certain line and the pitch of the note on that line. These symbols were called *clefs*.

Music for the bass is written in the *bass clef*. The symbol for the bass clef is derived from the Old German way of writing the letter F. Sometimes the bass clef is called the *F clef*, because the two dots surround the 4th line of the staff to show it is the note F.

You may want to use this simple trick to remember the notes.
On the lines: **G**reat **B**ig **D**ogs **F**ight **A**nimals On the spaces: **A**ll **C**ows **E**at **G**rass

Measures (Bars)

Music is also divided into equal parts called *measures* or *bars*. One measure is divided from another by a *bar line*.

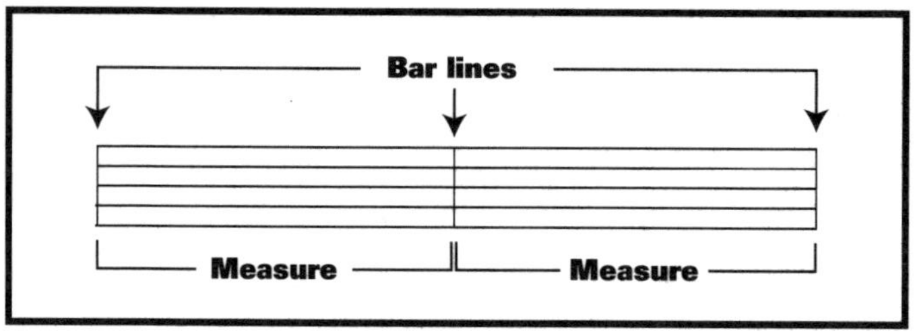

Reading TAB

All the music in this book is written two ways: in traditional music notation and in *TAB*.

Below each traditional music staff you'll find a four-line TAB staff. Each line represents a string of the bass, with the highest, thinnest string at the top and the lowest, thickest string at the bottom.

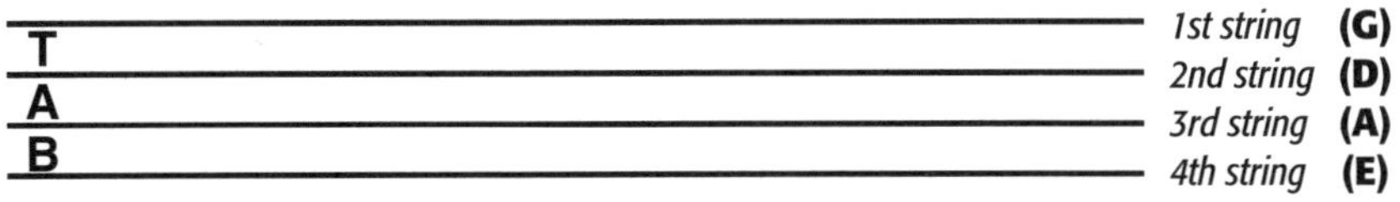

Numbers placed on the TAB lines tell you which fret to play.
A zero means to play the string open (not fingered).

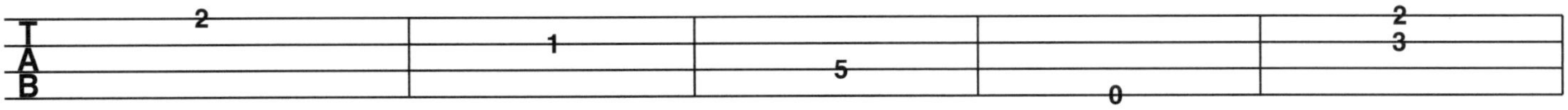

1st string 2nd fret | **2nd string 1st fret** | **3rd string 5th fret** | **4th string open** | **1st string, 2nd fret 2nd string, 3rd fret**

By glancing at the TAB, you can immediately tell where to play a note. Although you can't tell exactly what the rhythm is from the TAB, the horizontal spacing of the numbers gives you a strong hint about how long or short the notes are to be played.

Counting Time

Three Kinds of Notes

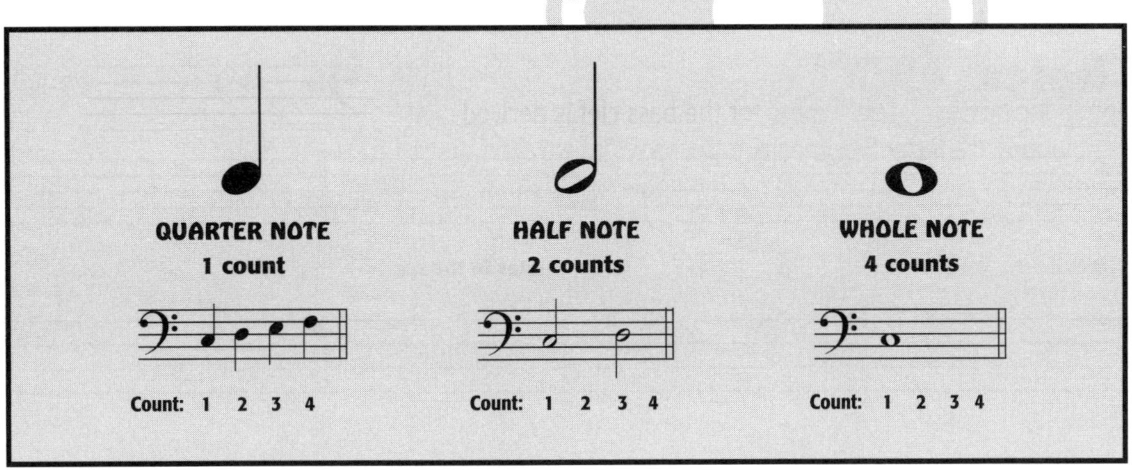

Time Signatures

Each piece of music has numbers at the beginning called a *time signature*. These numbers tell us how to count time.

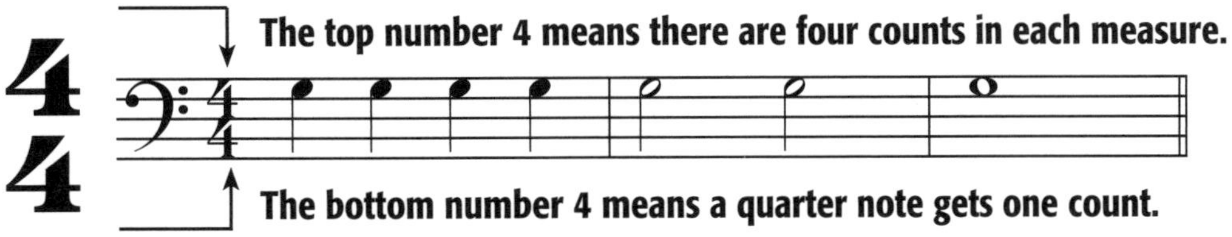

Notes on the First String G

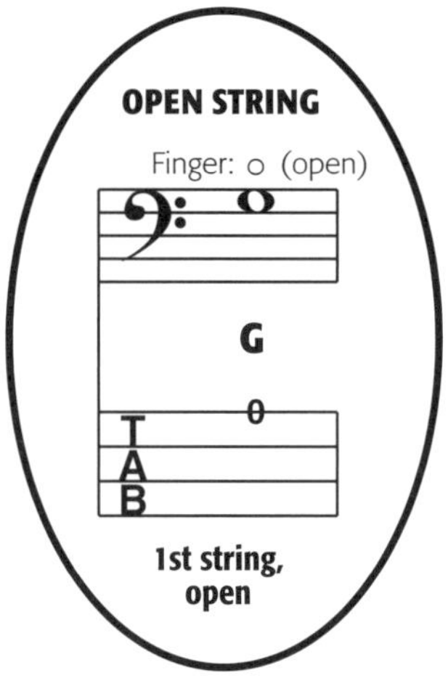

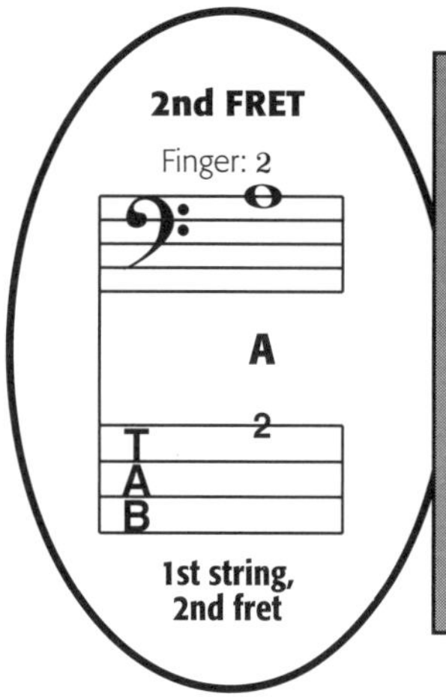

Playing Quarter Notes

Track 2

A double bar line indicates the end of a piece.

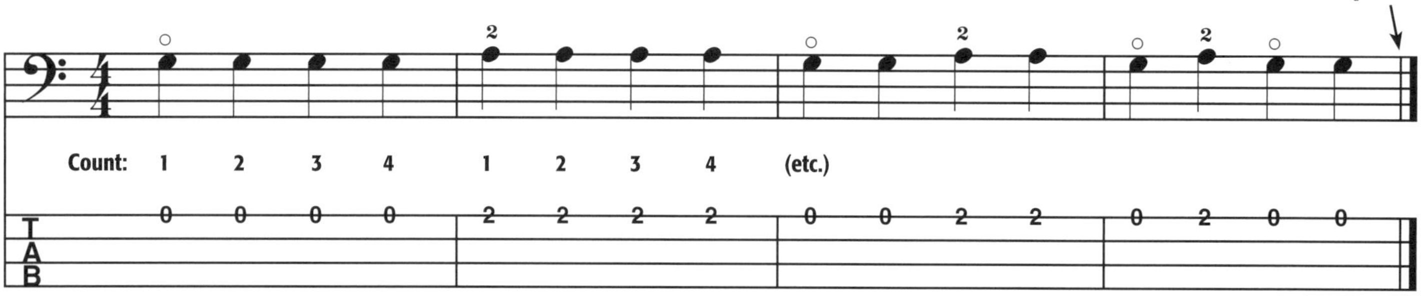

Playing Half Notes

Track 3

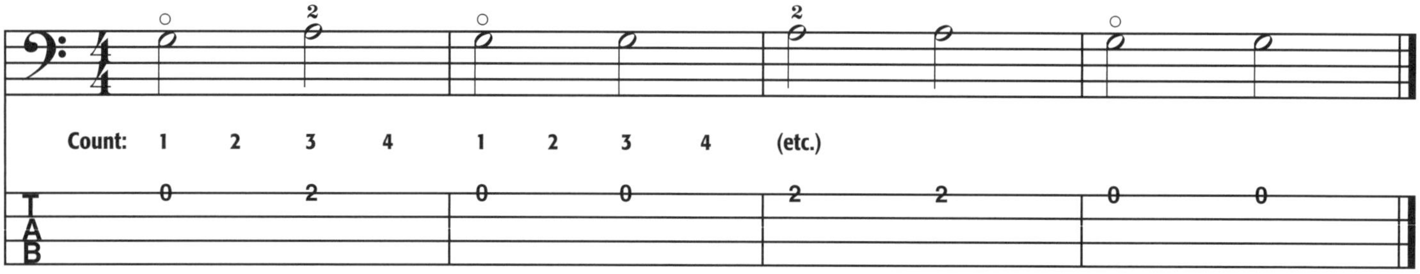

Playing Whole Notes

Track 4

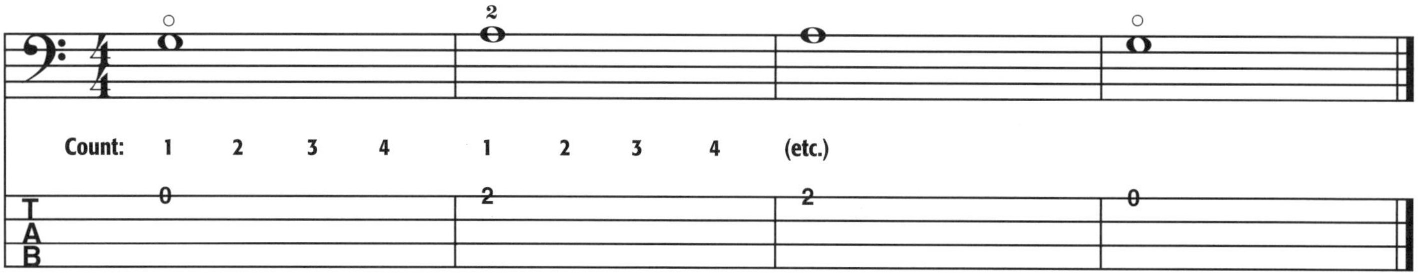

Right Place, Right Time

Track 5

Continue to next line without stopping.

The double bar line indicates the end of the piece.

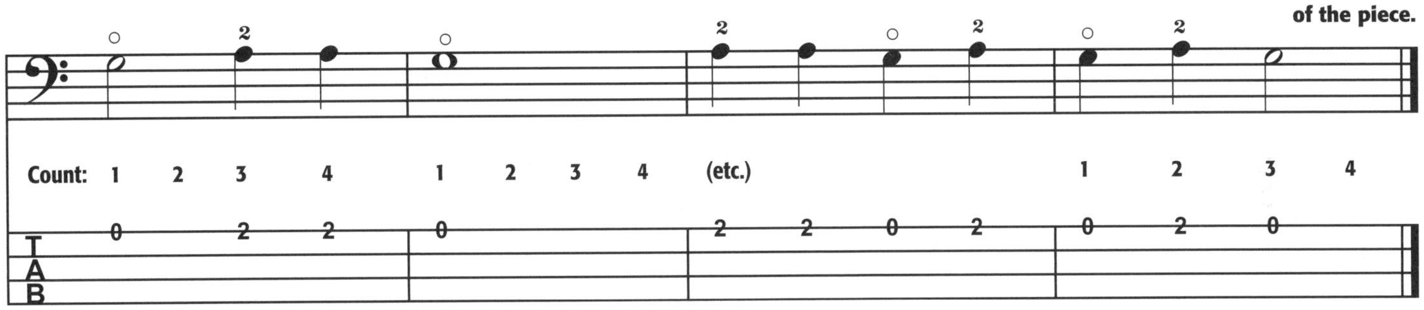

Melissa Auf der Maur

Hole, Smashing Pumpkins, Auf der Maur

"The Bass: The Mother of All Instruments.

From the place in which the bass sits in the music, to the role of the bass player in a band, it is the most emotional and sensual part of music. You don't watch the bass, or hear the bass, you FEEL it. The subfrequencies hit you in the subconscious, the most magical place to be and most profound place to connect. At 19 years old, my gut brought me to the bass. It wasn't a conscious decision, but now, 13 years into my elaborate relationship with the bass, I understand why I was drawn to it: It is my female instict to explore emotions and sensuality.The Bass is a She and so are We! My bass has been the most exciting partner of my life. She has brought me around the world and into the hearts of so many amazing people. Thank you, my favorite four strings!"

Photo © Mitchell Gerber/CORBIS

Notes on the Second String D

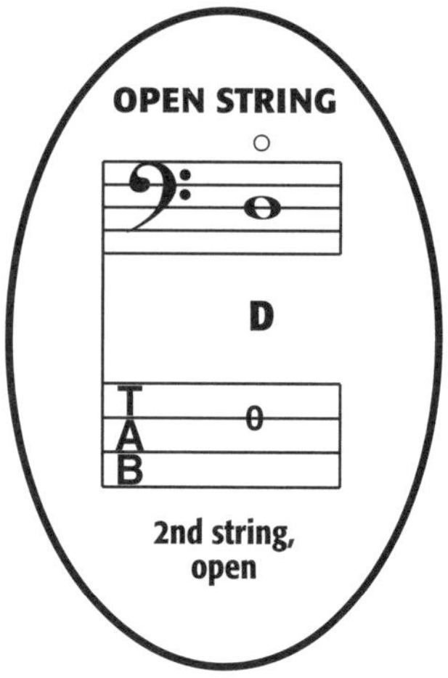

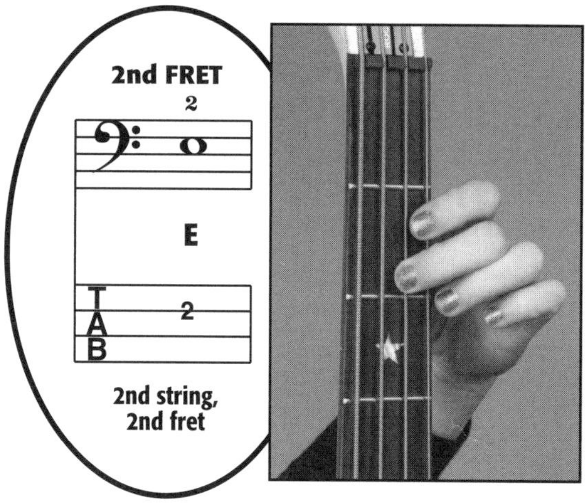

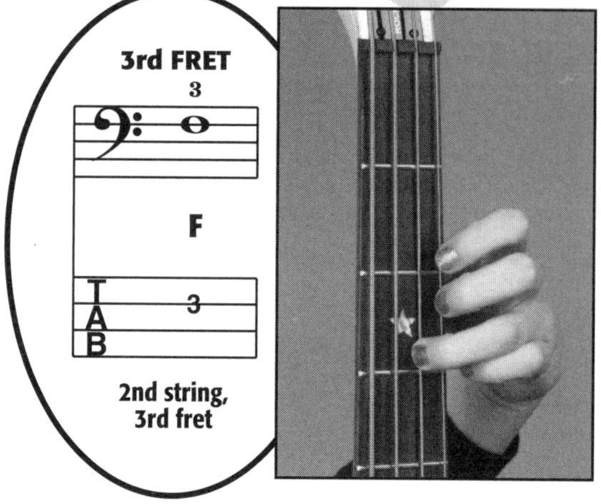

If you have trouble playing with the third finger alone, try adding the fourth finger until you build up strength in your third.

Climbing D Stairs

Track 6

See Saw on D

Track 7

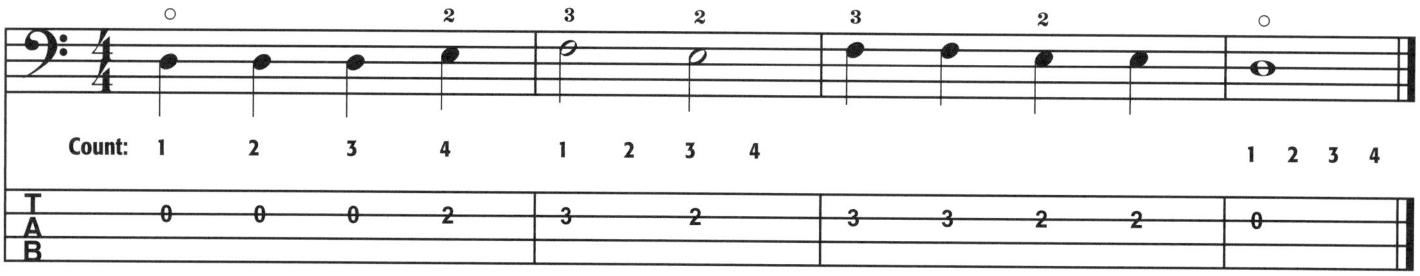

Carol Kaye

One of the most in-demand studio musicians since 1958, Carol Kaye may be the most influential bassist of all time. Her unique playing styles are heard on a remarkable number of hits recorded by popular artists like the Beach Boys, Ray Charles, Johnny Mathis, Nancy Sinatra, Glen Campbell, Henry Mancini, Sonny & Cher, Quincy Jones, Joe Cocker, Ike and Tina Turner, Mel Torme, and Frank Zappa. Her numerous movie and TV credits range from shows like Mission Impossible, Hawaii 5-0, the Thomas Crown Affair, Kojak, and Ironside to the Brady Bunch, Addams Family, Room 222, Wonder Woman and Guess Who's Coming to Dinner. In addition to her extraordinary experience as a performing musician, she has written numerous bass tutoring books and taught hundreds of students how to play.

Combining Notes On the G & D Strings

Two-String Warm-up

Track 8

Here is a great daily warm-up exercise that uses the notes you have learned so far.

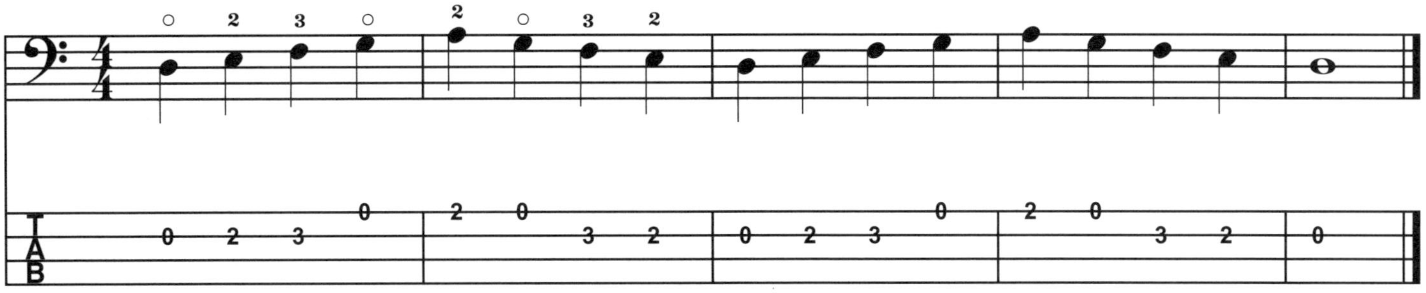

Surfer Girl in Blue

Track 9

Here is a great bass line to use when playing a D minor blues.

* Chord symbols that are placed above each staff may be used for a duet. Have a friend or teacher play the chords on the guitar or keyboard while you play the bass line, or play along with the audio track on the CD. Many of the tunes in the rest of this book include chords for duets.

Notes on the Third String A

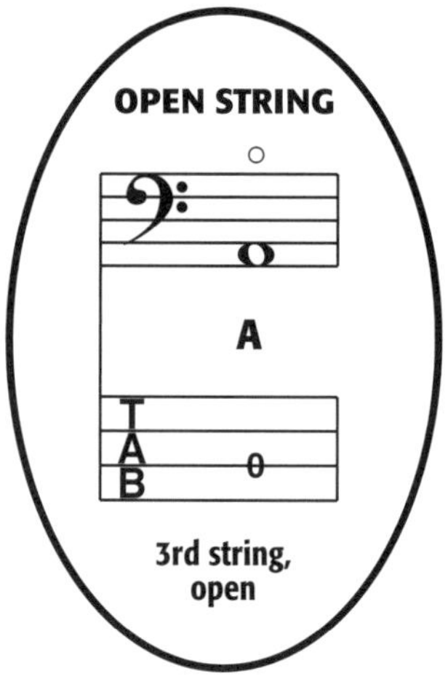

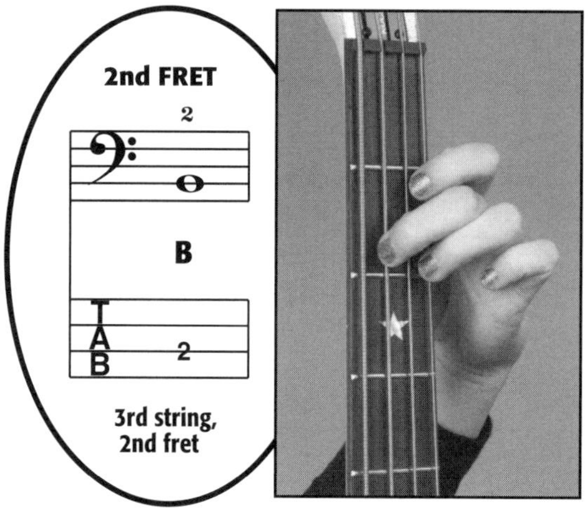

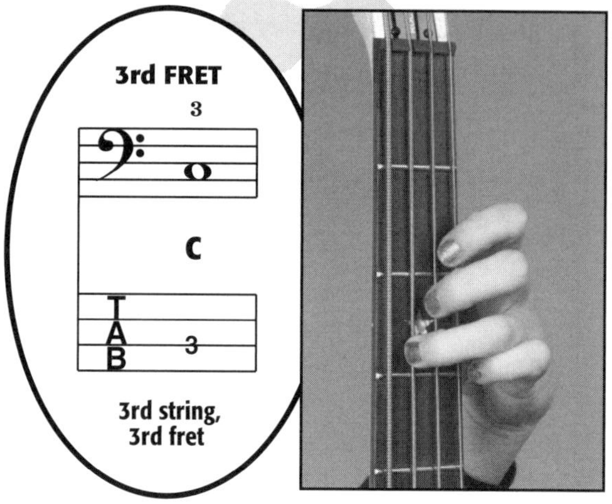

Up-Stems & Down-Stems

Until now, all notes have been written with the stems pointing down.
To make music look neater, down-stems *and* up-stems are used.

Notes above or on the middle line have stems pointing down.

Notes below the middle line have stems pointing up.

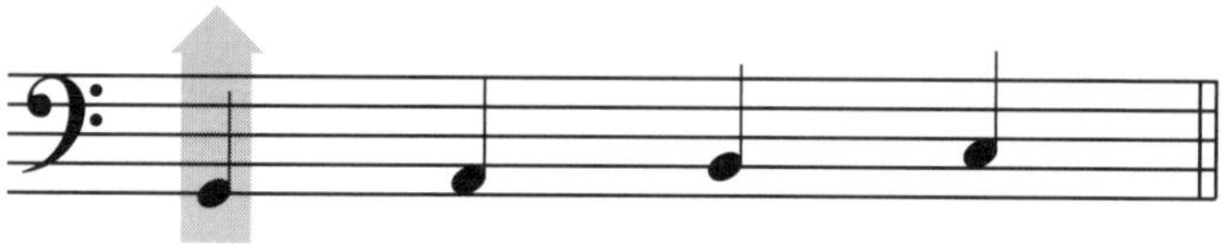

A Beautiful Stem

Track 10

Lovely A

Track 11

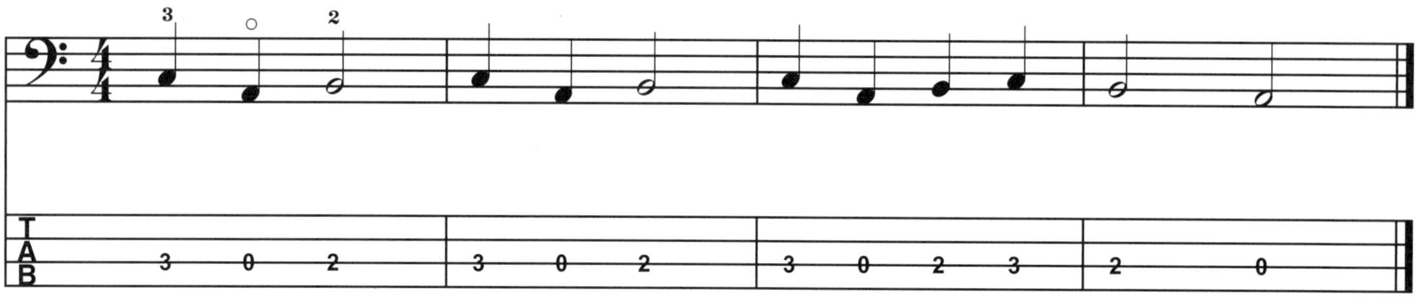

The A Natural Minor Scale

Track 12

A *scale* is a set of eight notes in alphabetical order arranged according to a specific pattern. Scales that follow the same pattern have a characteristic sound that is distinctly different than that of other types of scales.

The *natural minor scale* in A is also known as the *Aeolian mode*. This scale includes every note you've learned so far. Play it many times as part of a daily warm-up. Keep the beat steady and get a clean sound.

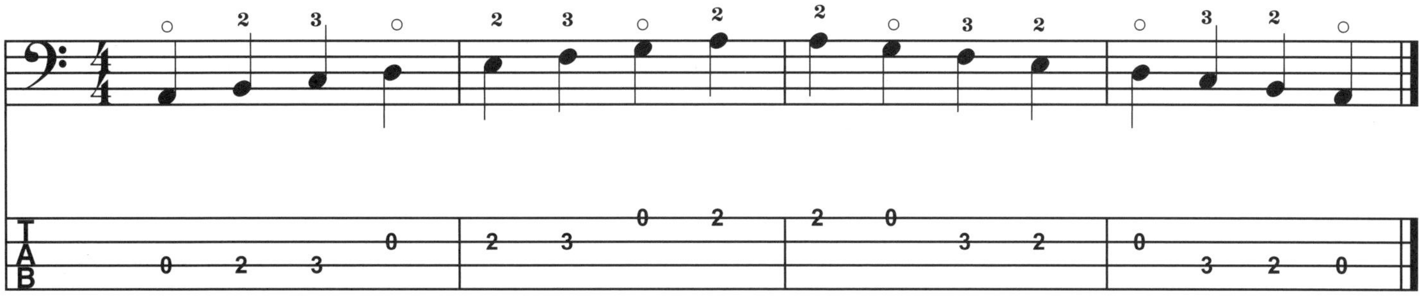

Girls Rockin', Naturally

Track 13

Sharps

A *sharp* sign ♯ placed before a note means to play that note one fret higher than usual. If the note is usually played on the open string, finger the sharp note on the 1st fret with the 1st finger.

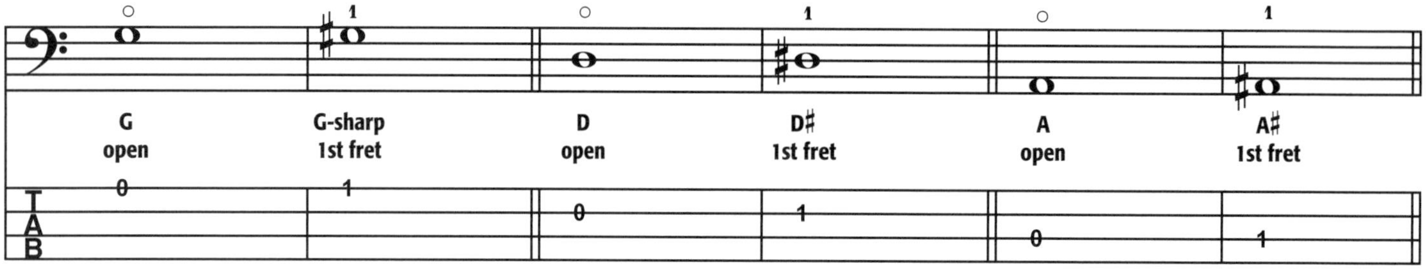

If the note is usually fingered, play the sharp note one fret higher.

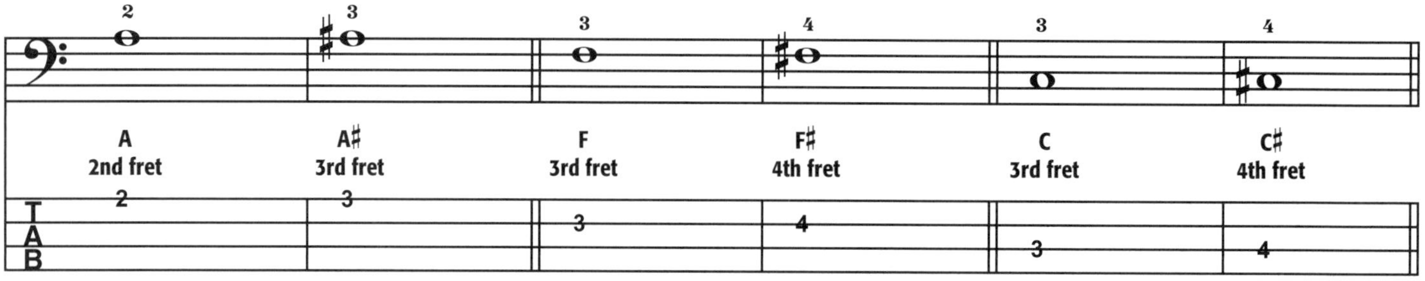

Since the note E♯ is the same as F, it is not used much. The same goes for B♯, which is the same as C.

Sharp Example No. 1 — Track 14

A sharp stays in effect for a whole measure.

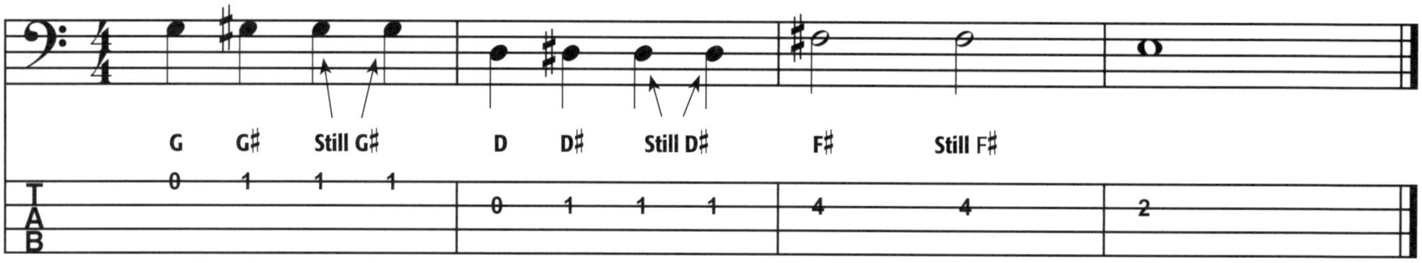

Sharp Example No. 2 — Track 15

The bar line restores a sharp note to its usual position.

Naturals — Track 16

A *natural* sign ♮ cancels a previous sharp sign in the same measure.

Notes on the Fourth Fret

You can play notes on the 4th fret with your 4th finger, or, if you do not have enough finger strength at this time, you can shift your 3rd finger up to the 4th fret.

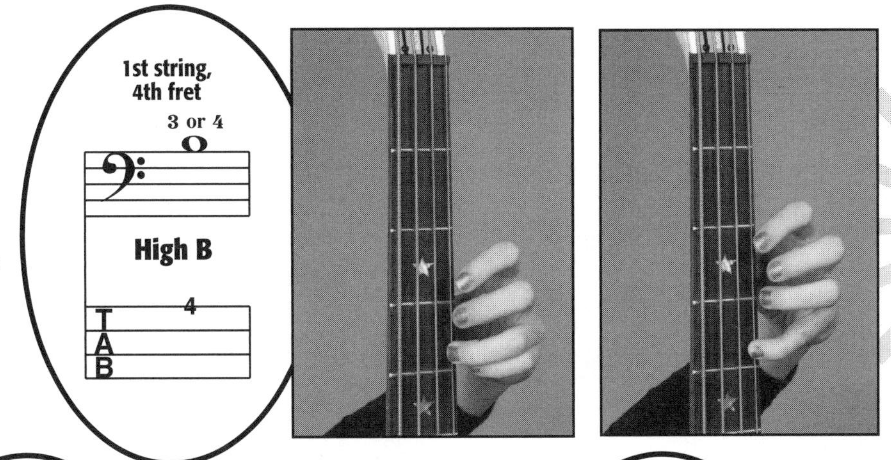

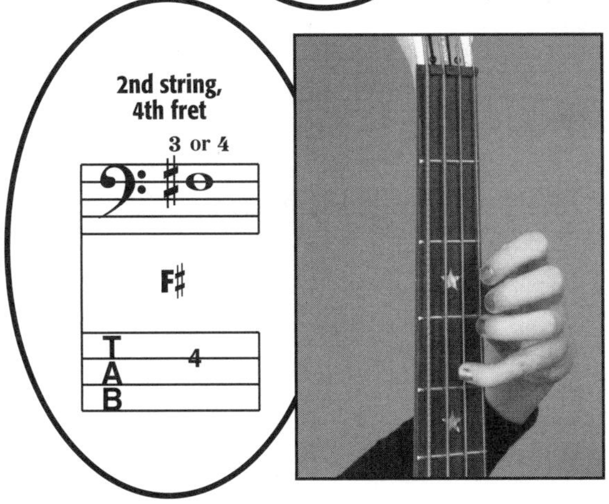

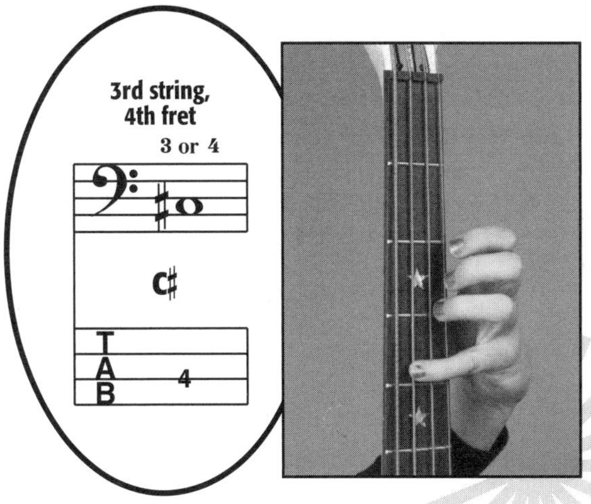

Practice these exercises that include notes on the 4th fret.

Fourth Finger Fiesta Olé

Track 17

Pinky Challenge

Track 18

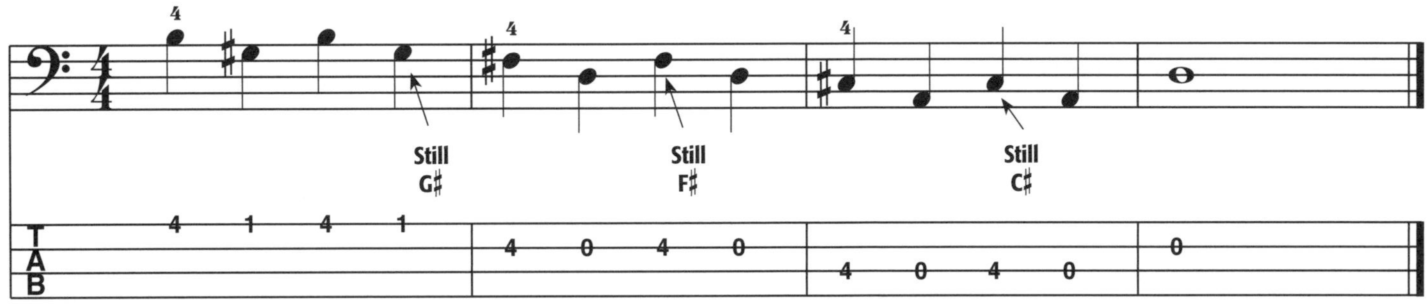

Notes on the Fourth String E

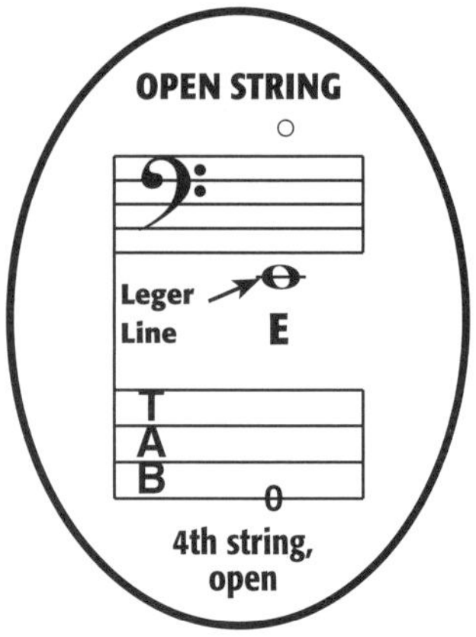

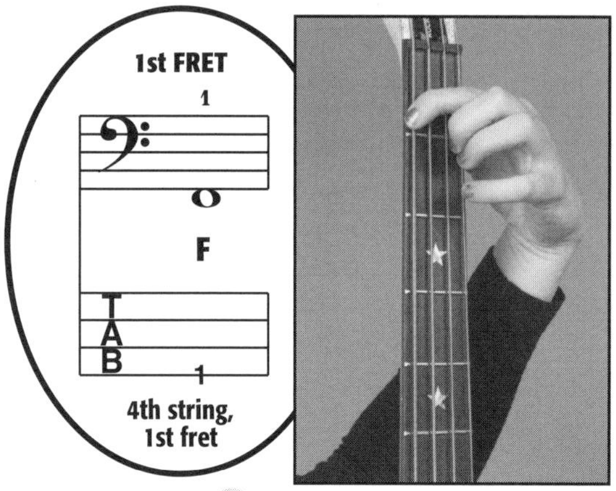

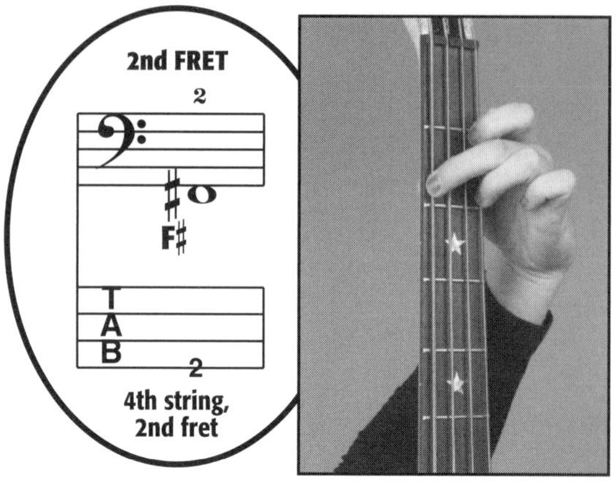

The short line that extends the staff downward for E is called a *leger line.* On a standard bass, only the low E requires a leger line below the staff.

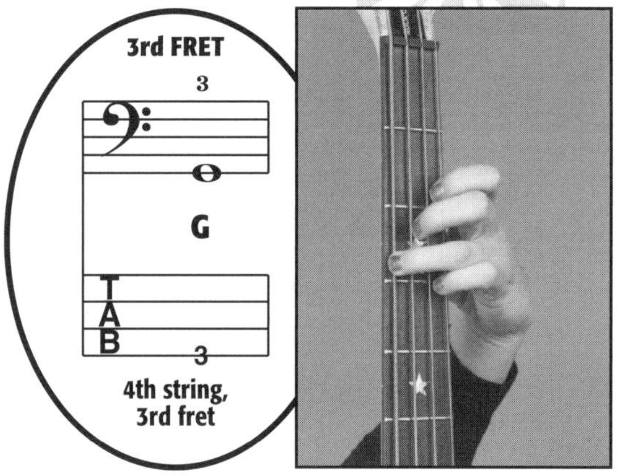

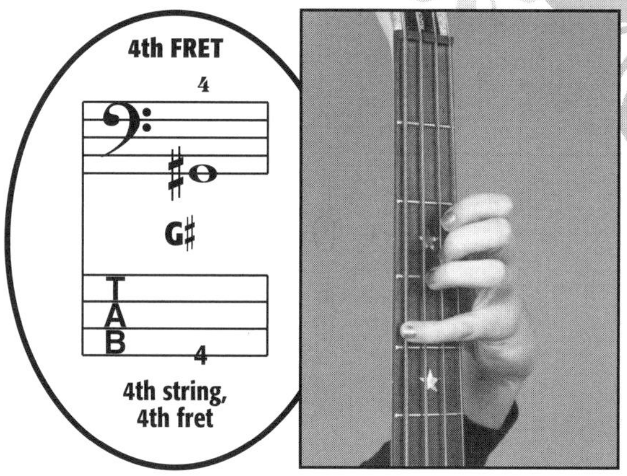

E String Fling

Track 19

The E string is the largest string on the bass, which makes it the most difficult to play. Be sure to press very hard with the left hand, close to the fret (without being right on it).

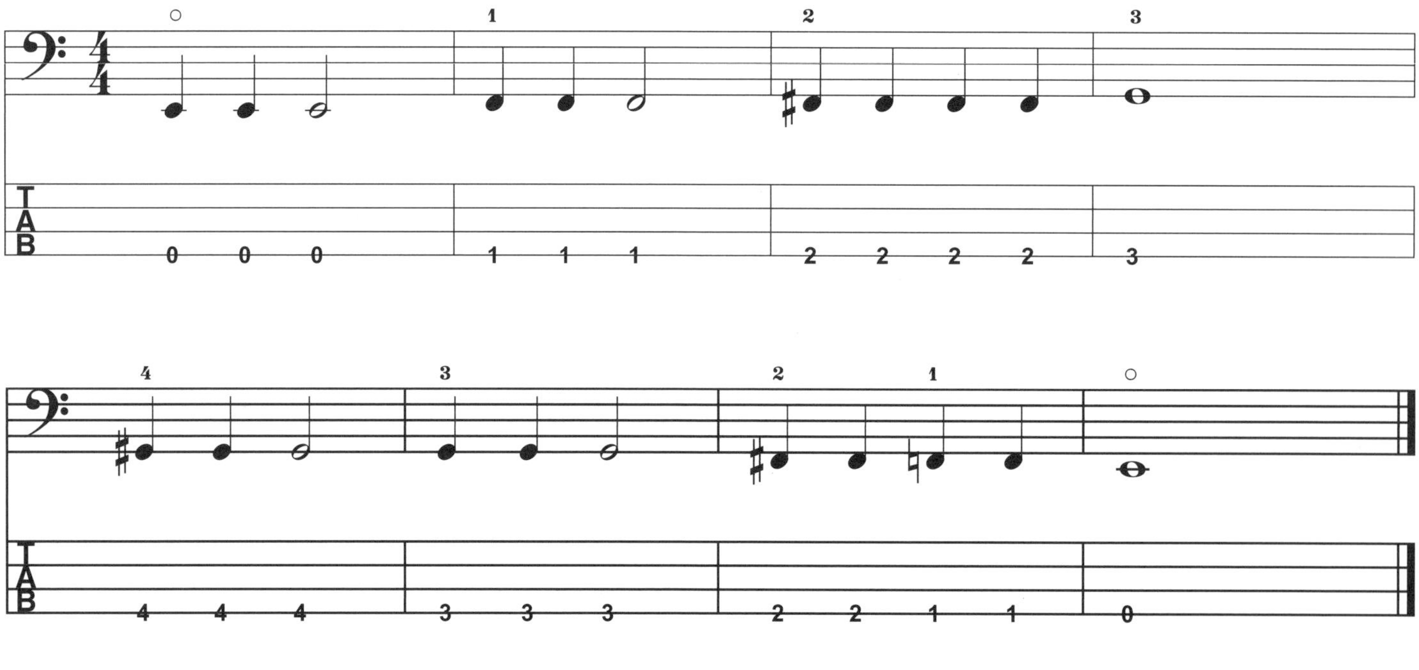

Note-Finding Review

Track 20

The following exercise uses every note you've learned so far.
Practice it until you can play without missing a beat.

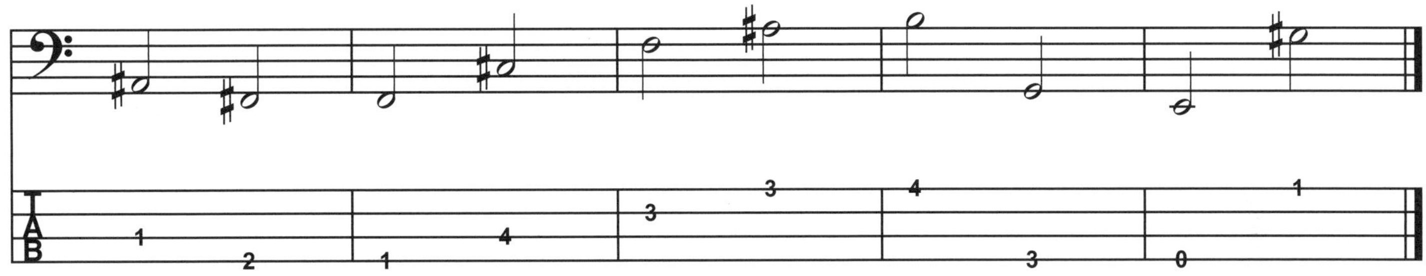

Walk All Over You

Track 21

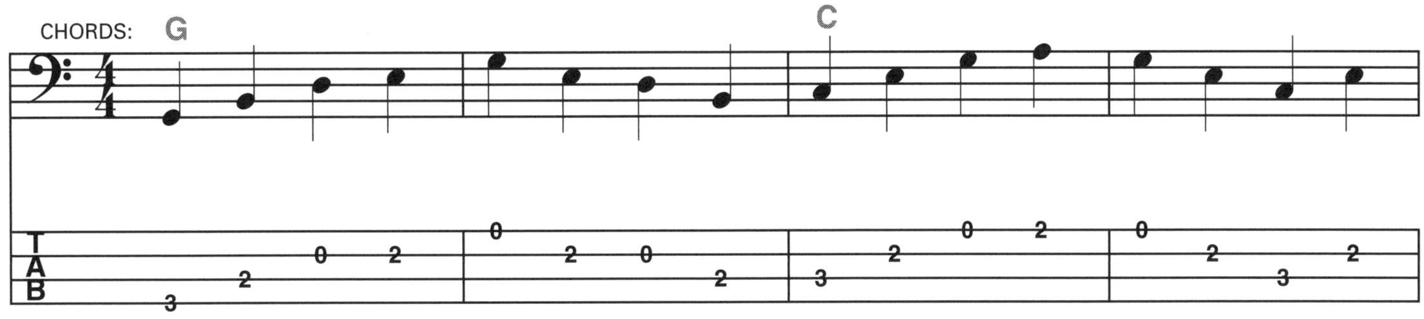

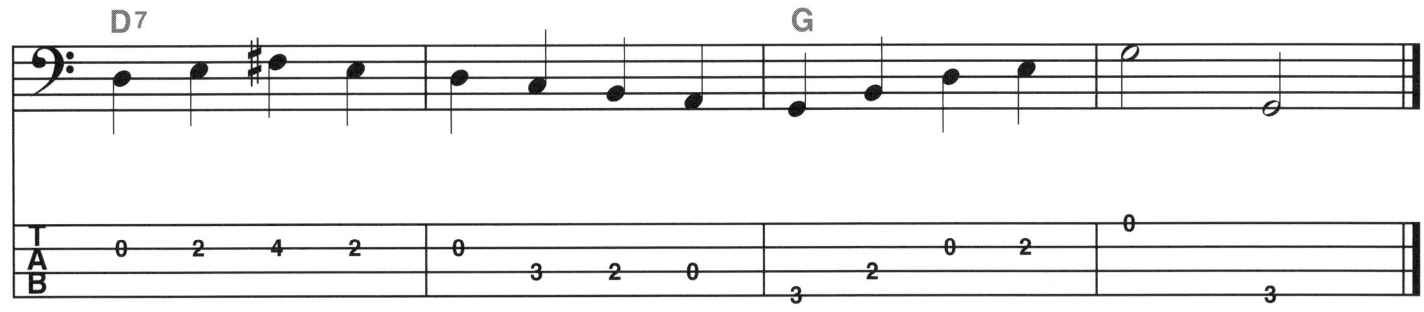

FLATS

A *flat* sign ♭ placed before a note means to play that note one fret lower than usual. For example, if the note is usually fingered at the 2nd fret, the flat note is played at the 1st fret; if the note is usually played at the 3rd fret, play the flat note at the 2nd fret.

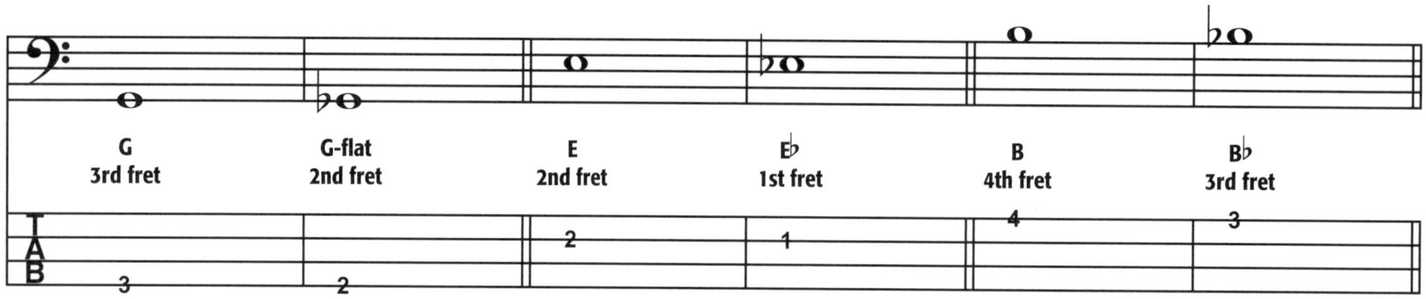

To flat an open-string note, play the next-lower string at the 4th fret.

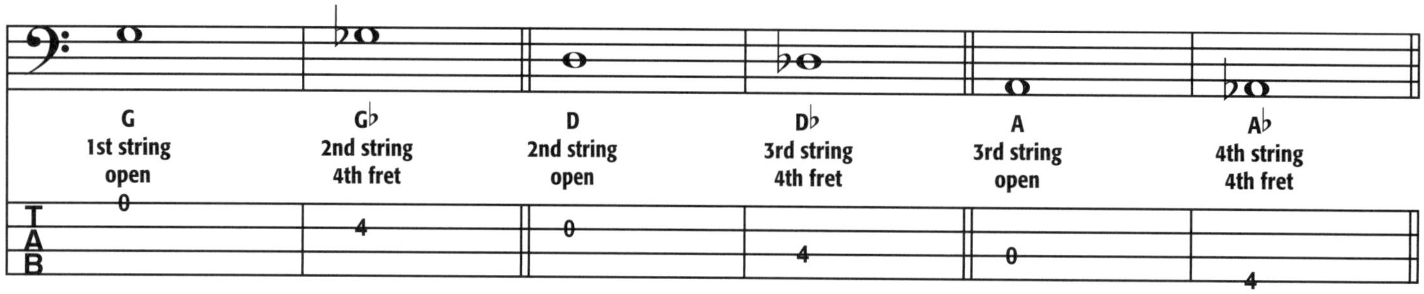

Just as for a sharp note, a bar line restores a flat note to its usual position. A natural sign ♮ cancels a previous flat in the same measure.

Trick or Treat

Track 22

Photo courtesy of Schecter Guitar Research

Sean Yseult

bassist: White Zombie, Rock City Morgue

"When I first moved to New York, I knew I wanted to be in a band. Because of punk music, I knew I could do it without being a pro at first, but it was still a little intimidating. My main inspiration was Ivy from the Cramps, and Joan Jett—even though they played guitar, they helped as role models in a world where there weren't many girls. Later, when we started White Zombie, metal head dudes would come up to me and say, "You and Cliff Burton are my favorite bass players!" It was really nice to have achieved my one of main goals in life—to be recognized as an equal, and break the "good for a girl" mold."

Nadja Peulen

Coal Chamber

Photo by Neil Zlozower

"I first started playing music in high school when I picked up the drums, the coolest instrument in music class. I realized I had a natural feel for it and a good sense of timing and rhythm. After jamming with some people for fun, I wanted to do some writing and thought about picking up the bass. For my 22nd birthday I got a bass from a friend and I learned some songs like "Iron Man" and "Smoke on the Water." I never took any bass lessons, but I am very determined when I want something, so I practiced a lot. A friend introduced me to a girl band that was looking for a bassist. At that time I wasn't very confident in my playing but I went down there to play with them anyways. I like to challenge myself and I figured, just go for it—what do I have to lose? Three months later I was playing my first shows in small clubs. After rehearsing regularly and playing gigs I became a better player, and two years later I was asked to audition for Coal Chamber. The rest is history!"

The Key of F Major

The F Major Scale

Track 23

A *major scale* is a series of eight notes in a specific arrangement of *half steps* (next fret) and *whole steps* (skip a fret). The pattern is always **W W H W W W H** (**W**= whole step, **H**= half step). The F major scale begins on F and contains a B♭.

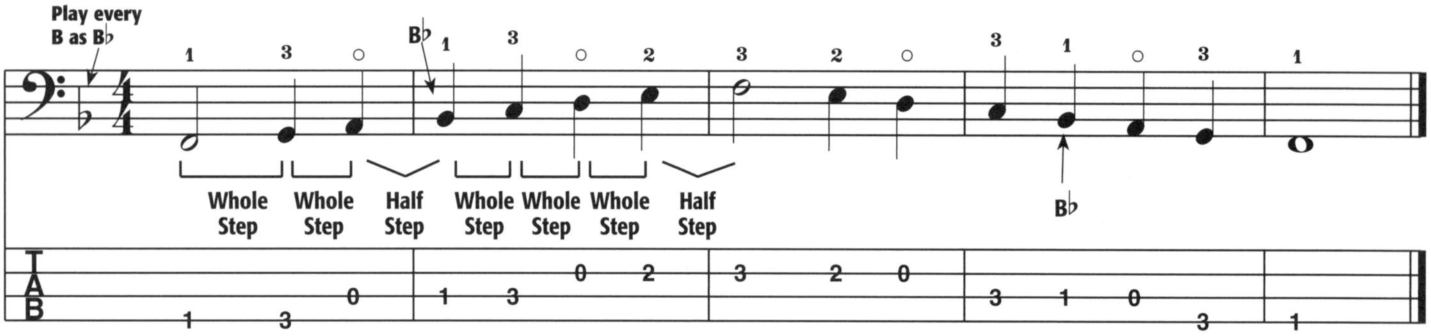

Key Signatures

Flats or sharps placed at the beginning of every staff line are known as a *key signature*.

A key signature of one flat (B♭) means to play every B as a B♭, unless preceded by a natural sign. It also tells you the music is in the *key of F major*. A *key* is kind of a musical "home base" from which the music departs and eventually returns. Notice that pieces in the key of F almost always end on the note F.

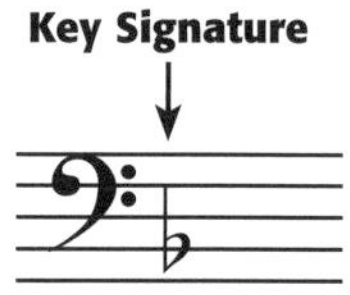

'50s Sock Hop in F

Track 24

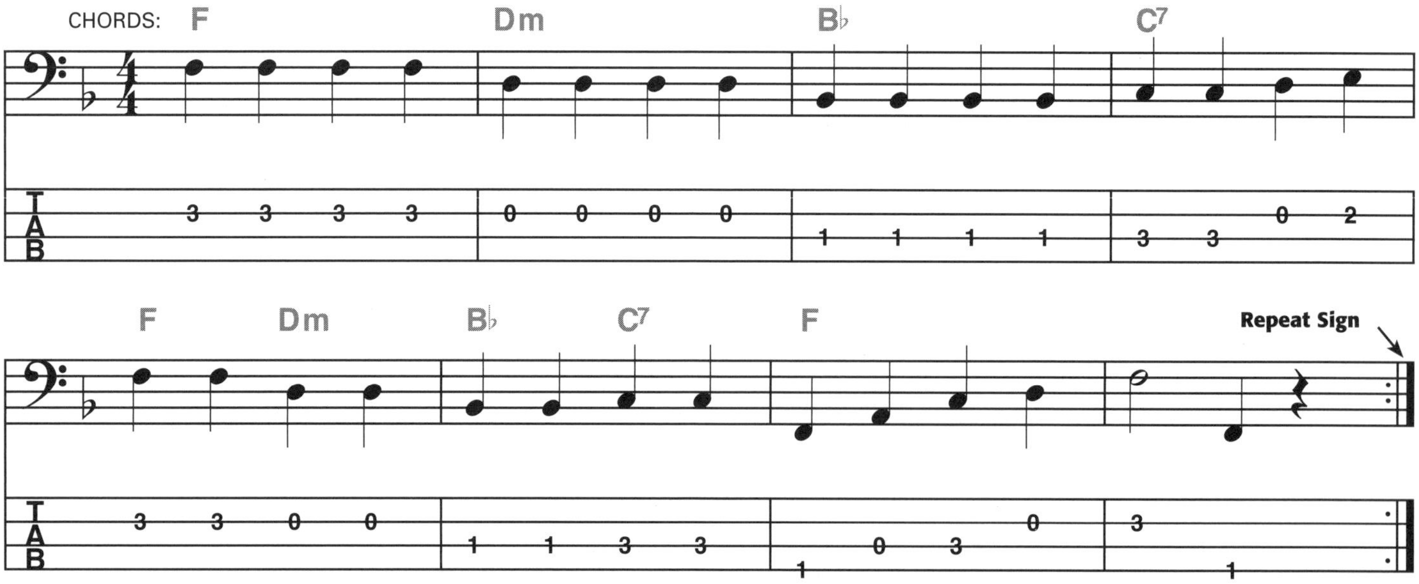

A repeat sign at the end of a piece means to go back to the beginning and play the entire piece again.

The Key of B♭ Major

A key signature of two flats (B♭ and E♭) tells you the piece is in the *key of B♭ major*. Unless preceded by a natural sign, all B's are played as B♭'s and all E's are played as E♭'s.

First practice the scale, then play the exercise.

The B♭ Major Scale

Track 25

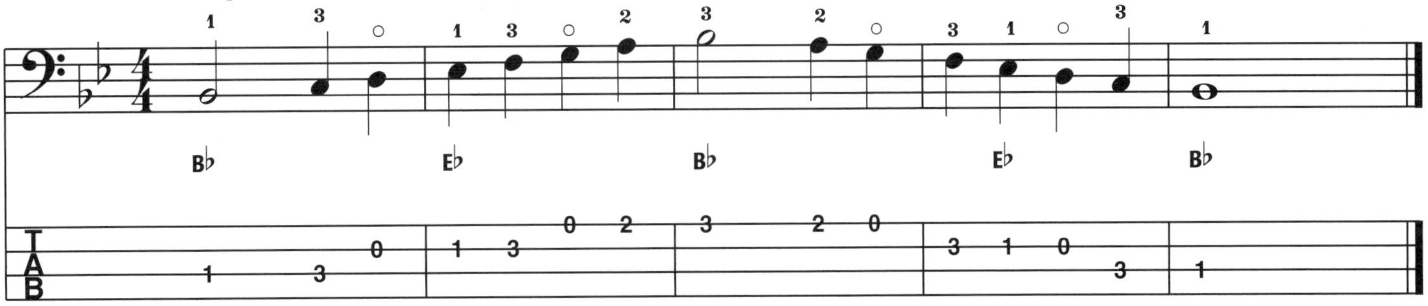

The Jazzy Ladylike Blues

Track 26

* **Flats, sharps and naturals that appear in a key but do not belong to that key (such as E♮ and A♭ in this piece) are called *accidentals*.**

Eighth Notes

Eighth notes are black notes with a flag added to the stem: 
Two or more eighth notes are written with a beam connecting the stems: 
There are two eighth notes per beat, and eight eighth notes per measure in $\frac{4}{4}$ time, which are counted **1 & 2 & 3 & 4 &**.

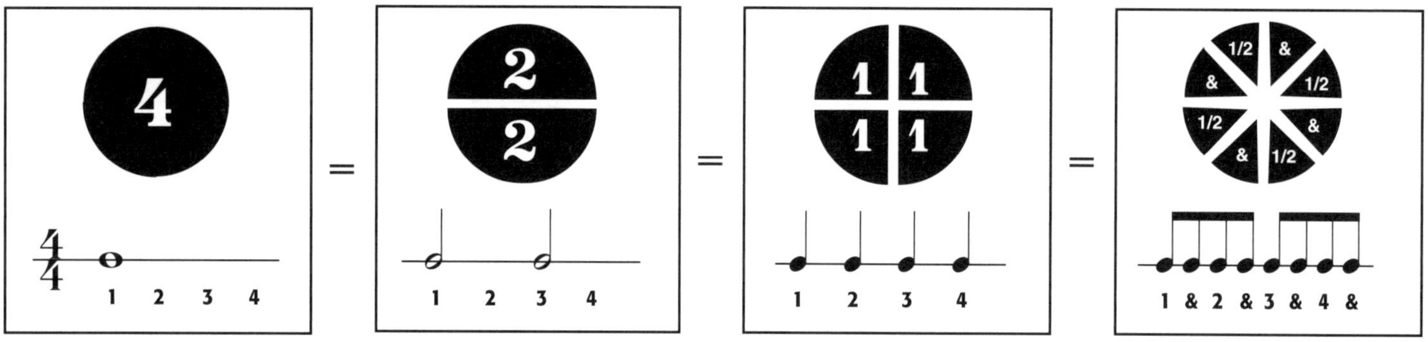

1 Whole Note = **2 Half Notes** = **4 Quarter Notes** = **8 Eighth Notes**

Eighth Notes on an Open String

Track 27

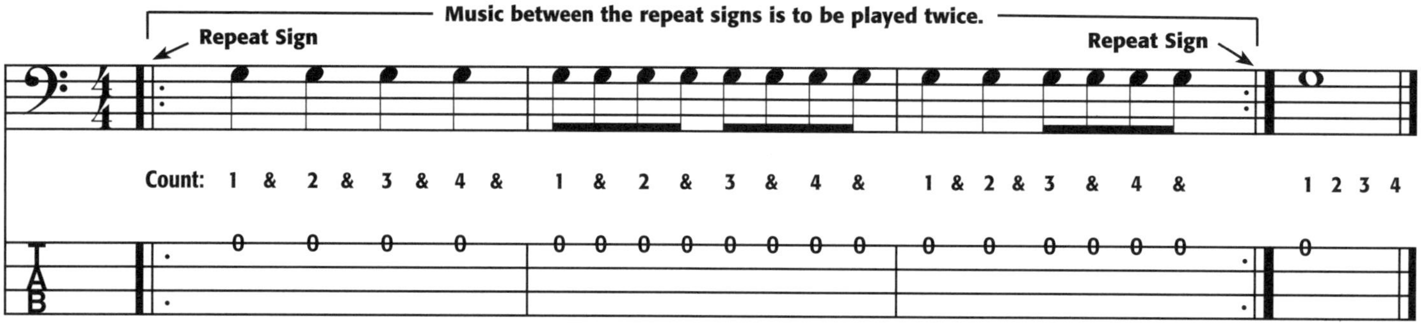

Eighth Notes on Three Open Strings

Track 28

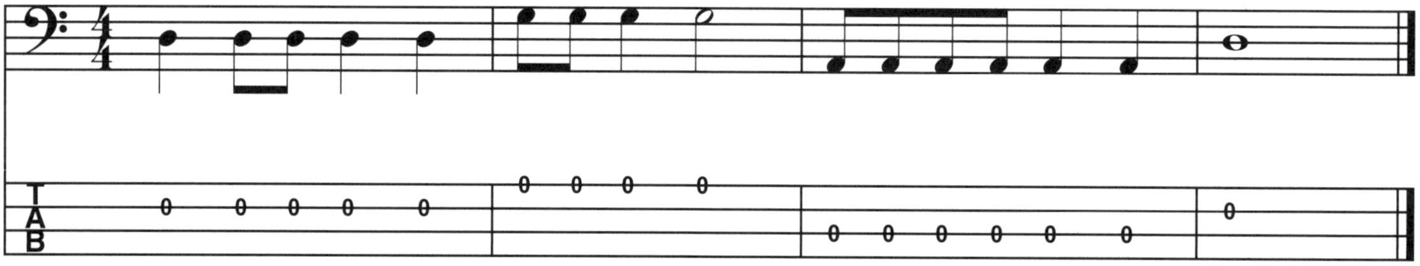

Eighth Notes with Fingered Notes

Track 29

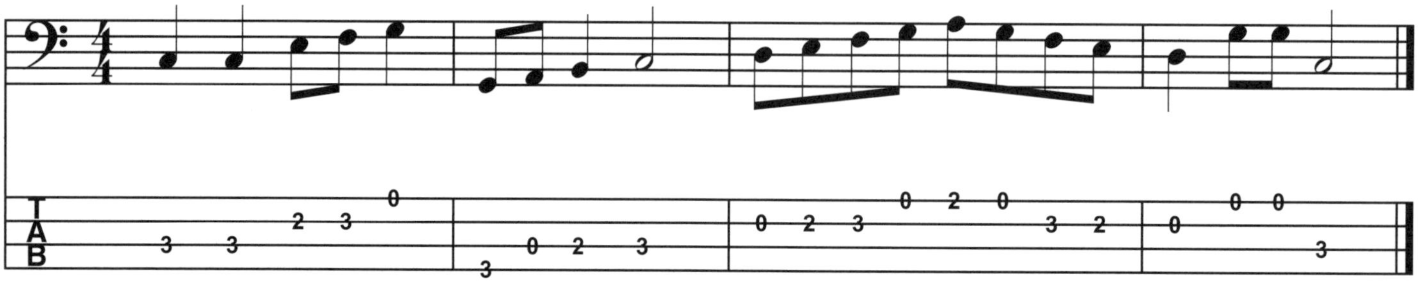

Rests

In music, a *rest* is a measured silence. It is important to get a clean sound when playing rests.

If the note before a rest is open, stop the vibration of the string with the fingers of the left hand.

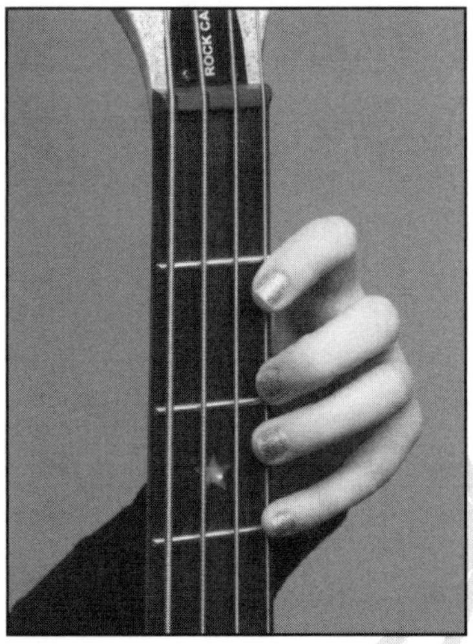

If the note is fingered, release the pressure on the string, but keep the finger touching it.

Three Basic Rests

QUARTER REST | **HALF REST** | **WHOLE REST**

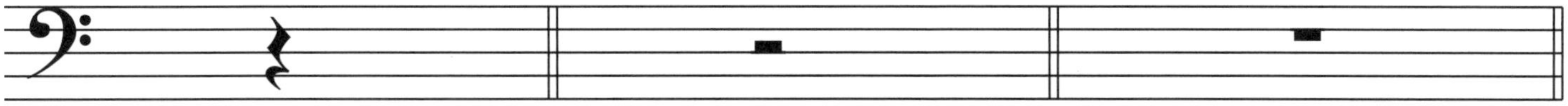

One beat of silence. | **Two beats of silence.** | **A whole measure of silence. (Four beats in $\frac{4}{4}$ time, three beats in $\frac{3}{4}$ time.)**

An easy way to remember the difference between the half rest and whole rest is to think of the whole rest as being longer, or "heavier," and so it hangs below the line. The half rest is shorter, or "lighter," and so it sits on top of the line.

Rest Exercise

Track 30

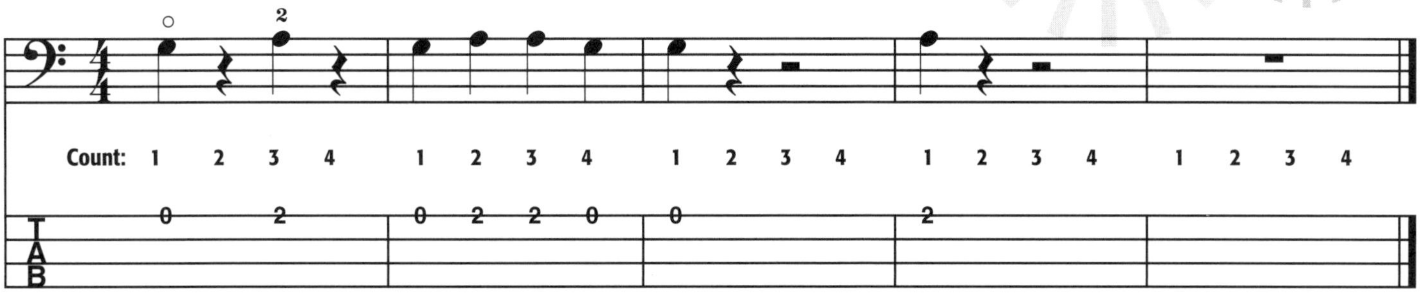

Jennifer Precious Finch

L7

"Playing the bass changed my life. It was the first thing that I every really wanted to do for myself, and not because my parents or school were making me. It gave me an opportunity to do something unique. It made me realize what the difference between being a fan and being a star was all about, not just in musical or career terms, but in all areas of my life."

Warm-ups in the Keys of F & B♭

The following exercises in the keys of F and B♭ combine eighth notes with other rhythms and make use of most of the notes you've learned so far. Serious students will want to add this page to their daily warm-ups.

Warm-up in F

Track 31

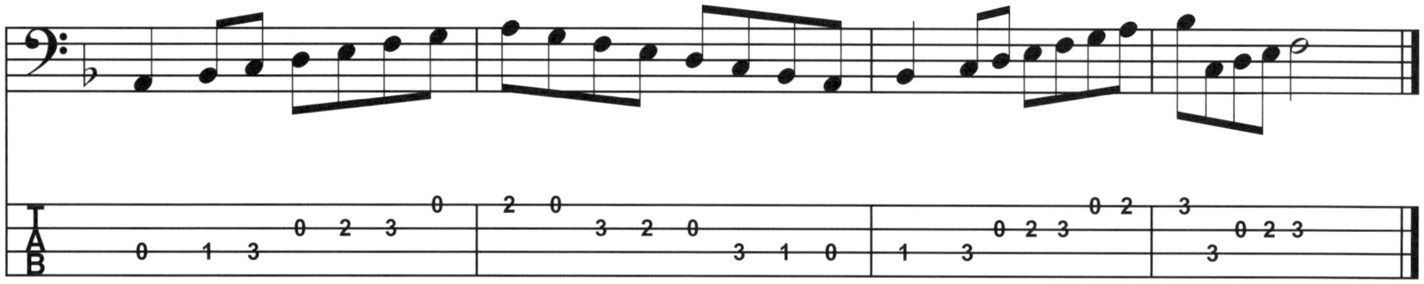

Warm-up in B♭

Track 32

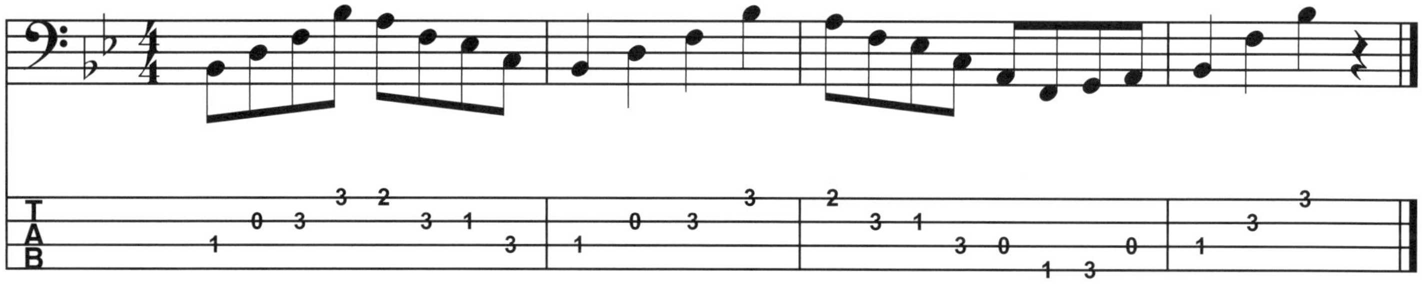

Riffs in the Keys of F & B♭

A *riff* is a short phrase, usually one or two measures long, that musicians use to fill in dead spots in the music and to add interest to their playing.

F Riff No. 1

Track 33

F Riff No. 2

Track 34

B♭ Riff No. 1

Track 35

B♭ Riff No. 2

Track 36

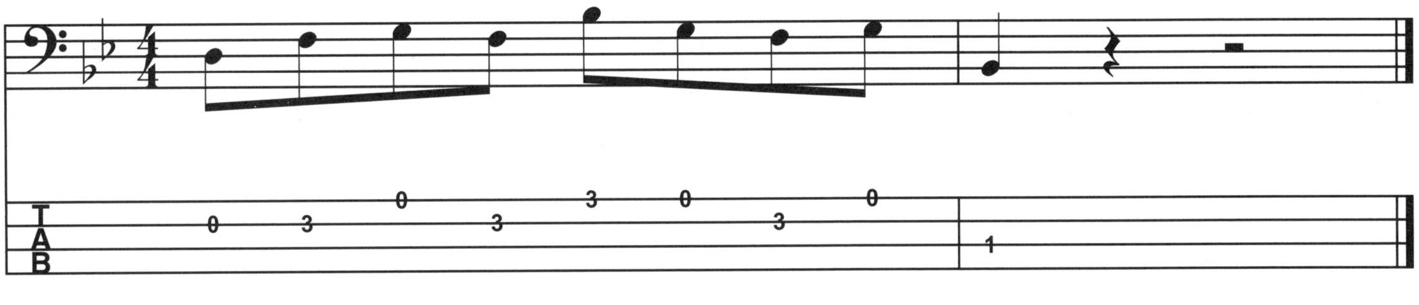

The Key of G Major

The key signature of one sharp (F♯) tells you a piece is in the *key of G major.* All F's are played as F♯'s unless preceded by a natural sign.

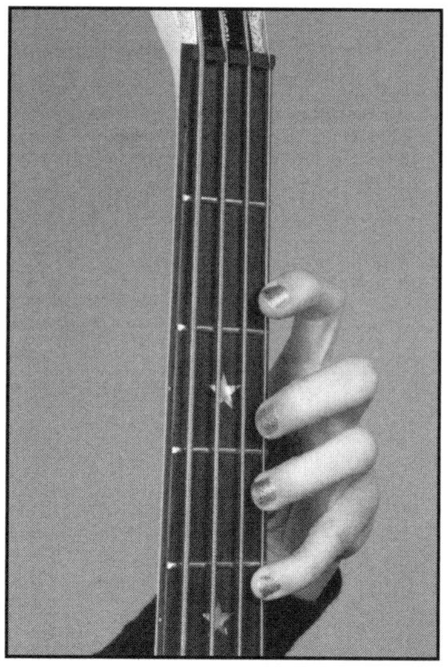

The hand in 2nd position.

The Second Position

All the notes you have played so far have been in *first position*. The version of the G major scale below is played in *second position*. This means that the left hand is shifted up the fingerboard so that the 1st finger plays notes on the 2nd fret, the 2nd finger plays notes on the 3rd fret, the 3rd finger plays notes on the 4th fret, and the 4th finger plays notes on the 5th fret.

The G Major Scale

Track 37

Learn the scale and add it to your daily practice.

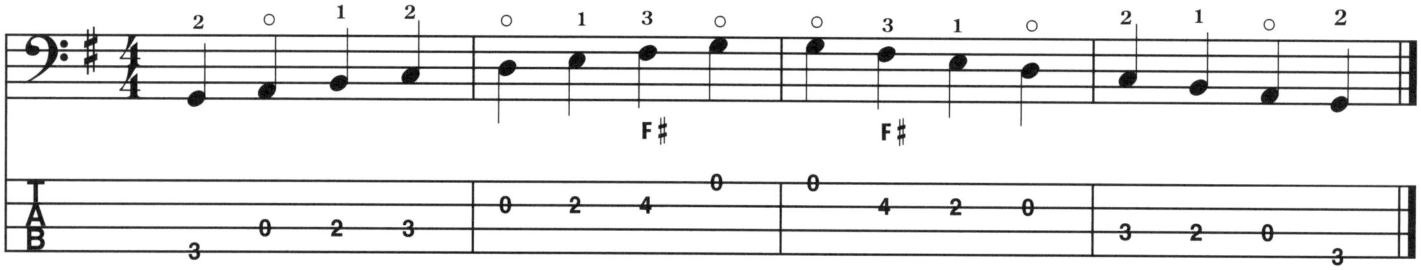

Good King Wenceslas

Track 38

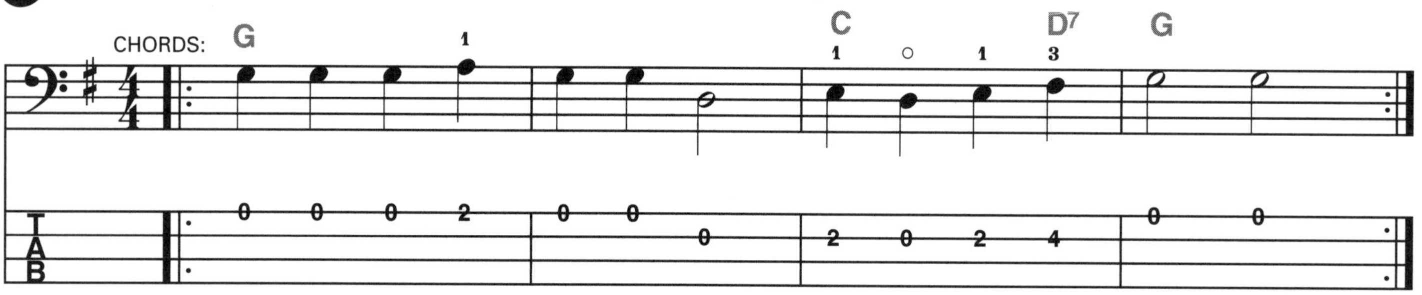

The Third Position

When playing in *third position*, shift the left hand so the 1st finger plays notes on the 3rd fret, the 2nd finger plays notes on the 4th fret, and the 3rd finger plays notes on the 5th fret.

The hand in 3rd position.

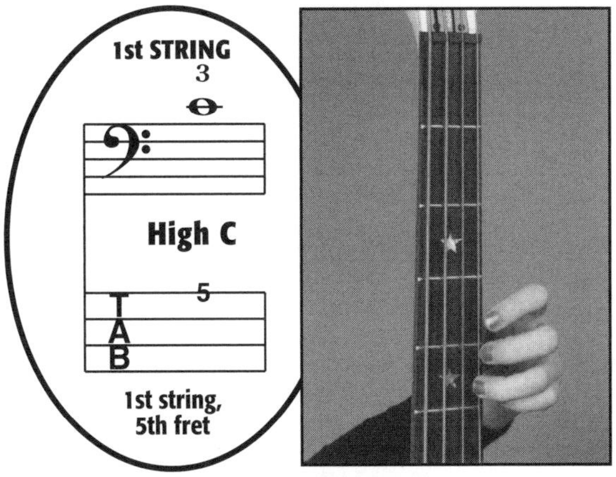

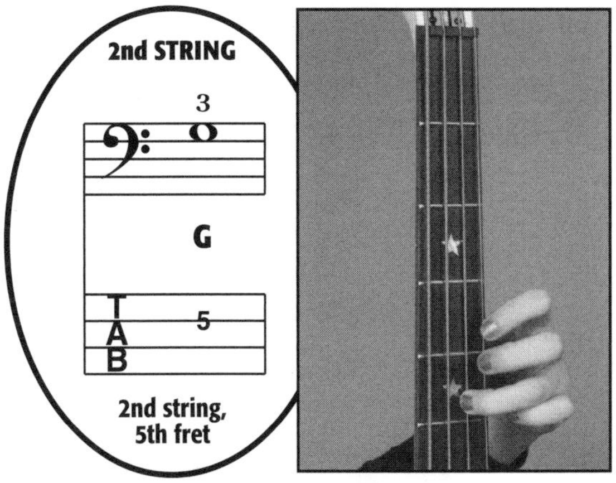

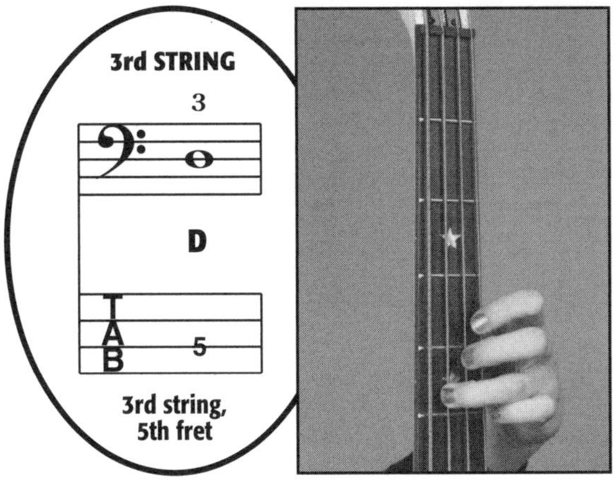

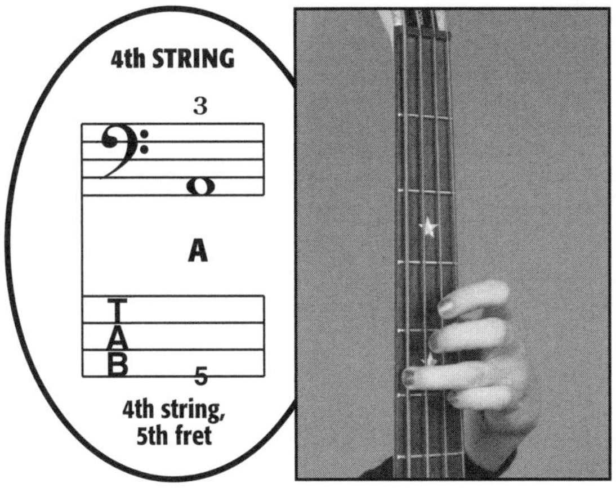

Notice that you now have alternate ways of playing the notes G, D, and A. Compare the following:

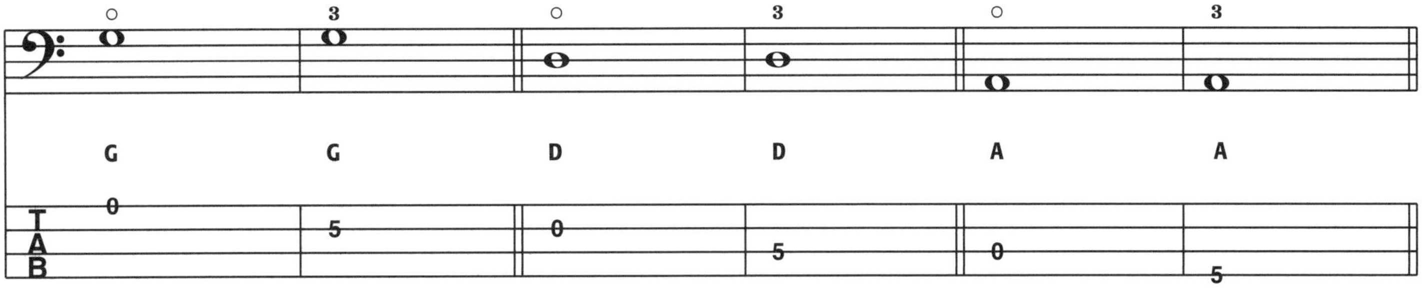

It is impossible to give a hard and fast rule about whether to use the open or fingered form of a note. Many players avoid using open strings altogether, but the best policy is to try a passage both ways and choose the form that is easier to play and produces the better sound.

For example, for the following passage, most players would find the fingering in the first measure easier to play:

The Key of C Major

A key signature with no sharps or flats tells you a piece is in the *key of C major*. All notes are played natural unless preceded by a sharp or flat.

As you practice this scale, notice that the fingering for some notes will change depending on your hand position.

The C Major Scale

Track 39

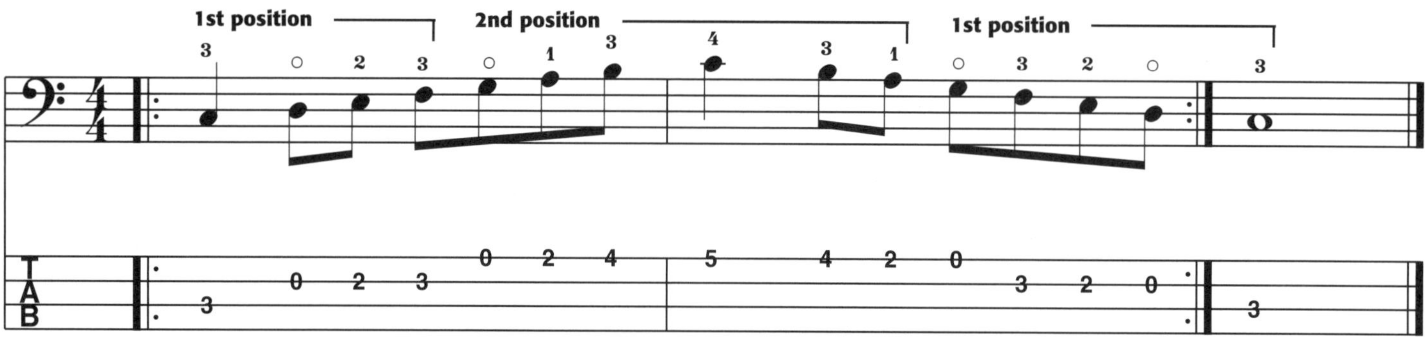

Bass Line for a Rocker Girl

Track 40

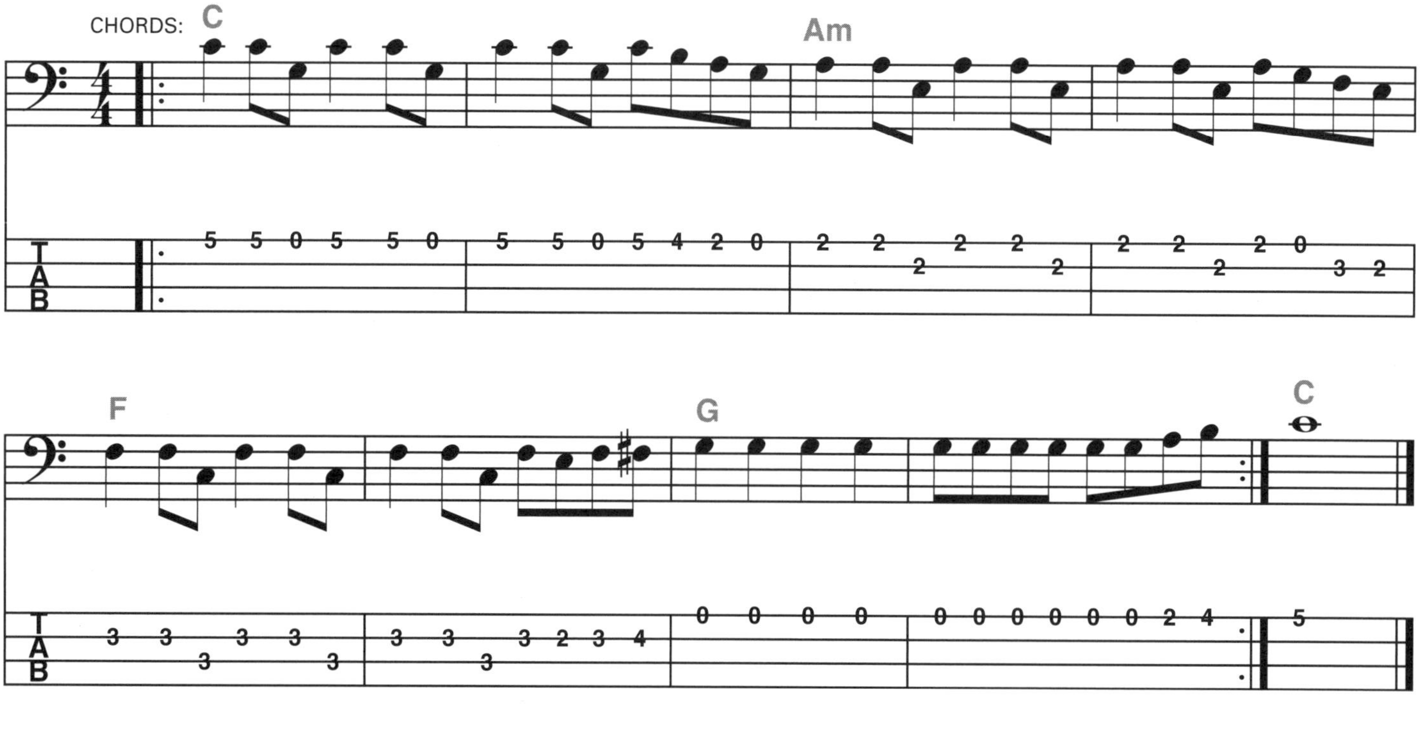

The Slide

Slide

To play a slide from a note to a higher note, pick the first note, then slide the fret finger up to sound the higher note without picking again.

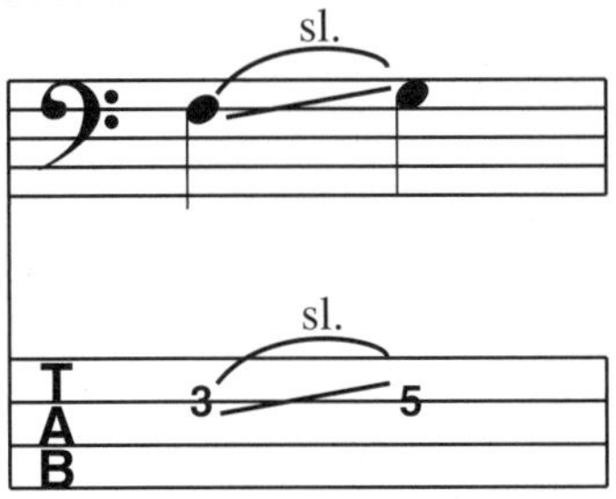

Slide Up

To slide up to a note, play the string as your fret hand slides up the neck to the written pitch.

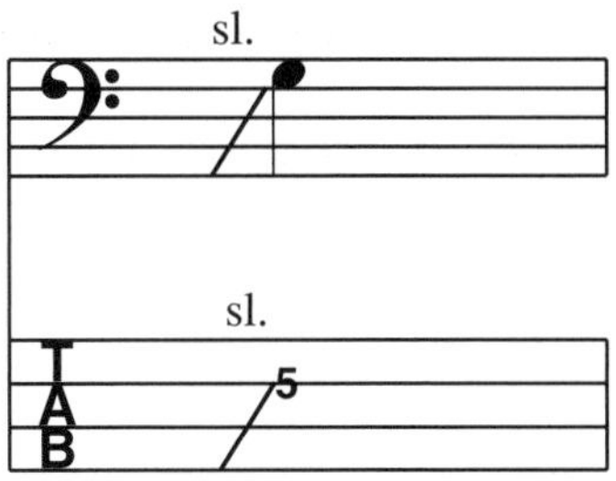

Below are some examples of slides used in country bass riffs.

Slide Example No. 1

Track 41

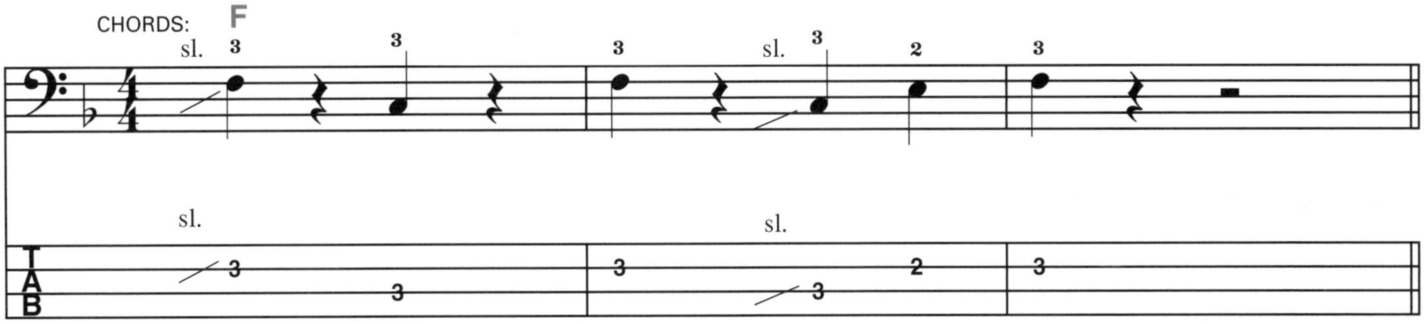

Slide Example No. 2

Track 42

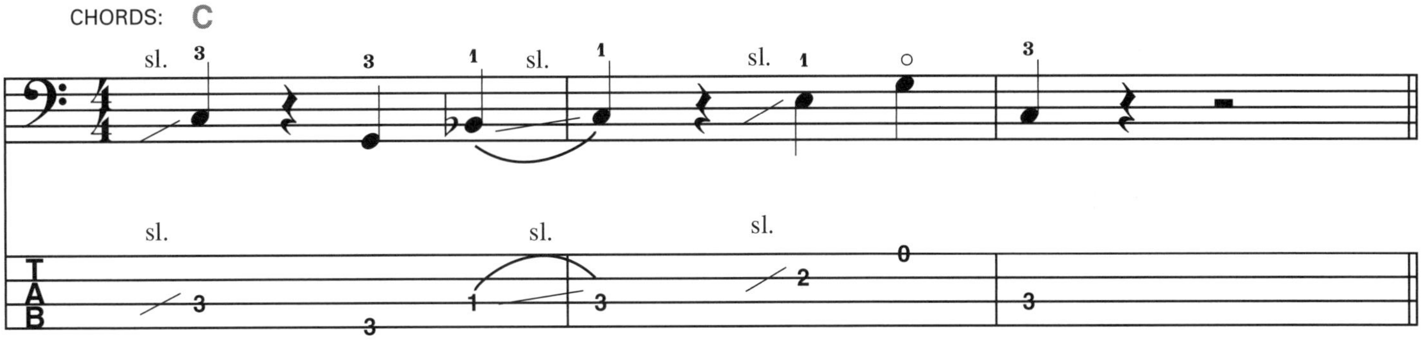

Accented Notes

An *accent* (>) means to play a note slightly louder than usual. The picking hand plucks the string harder for an accented note than for a non-accented note.

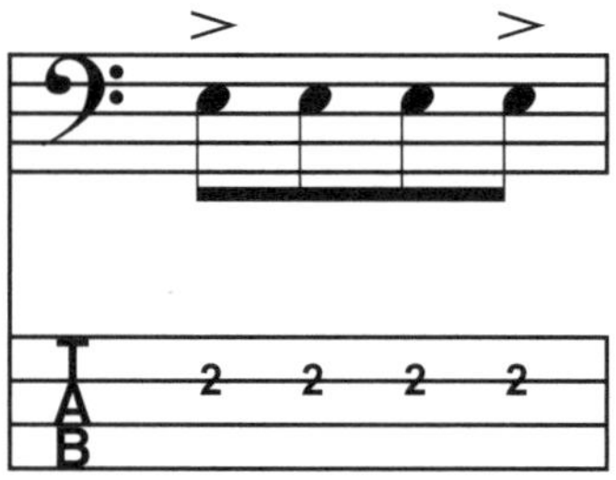

Below are examples of accented notes used in heavy metal bass riffs.

Photo © Ken Settle

Share Ross
Vixen

"Why did I start playing bass? Good question! I already played piano for several years and had tried drums, violin and guitar. Bass seemed like the next logical step to try, and lucky for me, it worked! There is something about carrying the low end of the song that I just love."

Accent Example No. 1

Track 43

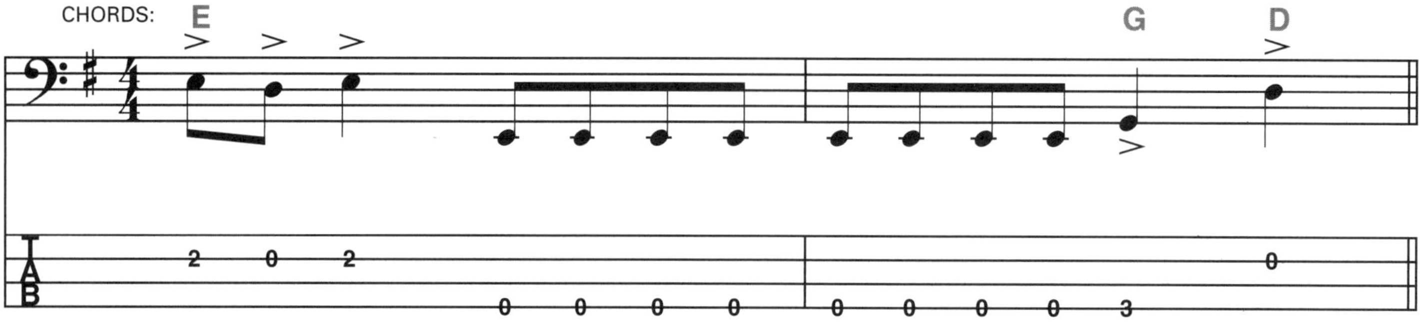

Accent Example No. 2

Track 44

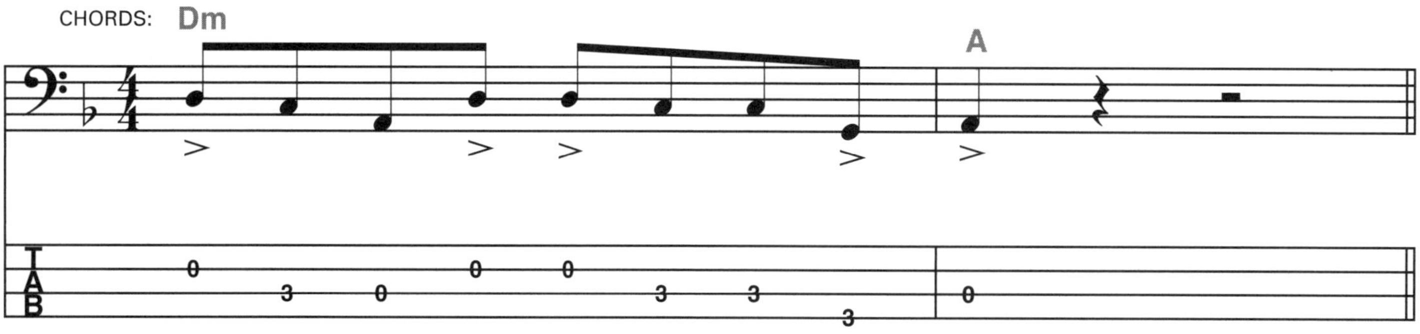

Photo © Markus Cuff/CORBIS

Kathy Valentine

The Go-Go's

"I'm not a traditional bass player, I don't think. My main instrument is guitar, and I play bass like I play guitar, with the same attitude and philosophy. My approach is this: Do what's right for the song—either play something that makes the song better, or play something that is simple and clean. Keep out of the way of the vocal melody, and listen to what everyone else in the band is doing and try to complement them, and make them sound better. In my opinion, bass is not an instrument for showing off, it's for musicians who really know how to play with other people."

Maya Ford

The Donnas

"I started playing bass when I was 12 because I loved music and I couldn't figure out how to play guitar; the strings were too small and I couldn't remember all the chords. So the bass was perfect because it was easier to play—no chords, big strings, and it was loud and I liked making noise. I was a big nerd obsessed with R.E.M. and wanted to be in a cool band like them. I had never met R.E.M., but they were my best friends. I wasn't very good at playing R.E.M. songs so I would simplify them. Then, when my band really got together and started playing in the garage, we learned some easier songs like L7 and Shonen Knife.

Photo by Sam Buffa

I think all the years I spent practicing and playing bass have kept me out of a lot of trouble. I guess it also helped me find some trouble, but whatever, it's fun. Music always helped me escape from my life. If I was bored or mad or tragically heartbroken, I would just put on an ABBA record. It's a cool feeling knowing that some kid out there can put on my album and get excited and inspired and maybe pick up a bass and try to play along. Playing bass rules!"

Ties & Syncopation

Ties

Ties are curved lines connecting two or more successive notes of the same pitch. When two notes are tied, the second one is not picked, but its time value is added to the value of the first note. In TAB notation, a tied note is indicated with parentheses—do not pick that note again.

Syncopation

Syncopation is a musical effect in which a note is *anticipated*, meaning it's played before its expected beat. Syncopation is critical to all types of music.

Example 1 below is not a syncopated rhythm. Each quarter note falls in the expected place, right on the beat. Examples 2–6 are various examples of syncopation.

Example 1

Track 45

Non-syncopated or "straight" version of the rhythm.

Example 2

Track 46

Beat 3 anticipated. (The third quarter note is played early, on the "&" of beat 2 rather than its expected place on beat 3.)

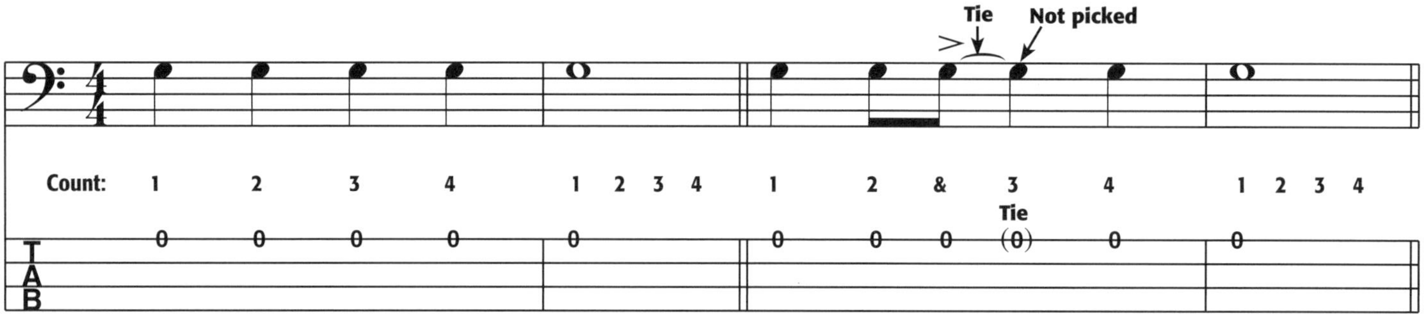

Example 3

Track 47

Beat 1 anticipated across the bar line.

Example 4

Track 48

Beat 2 anticipated.

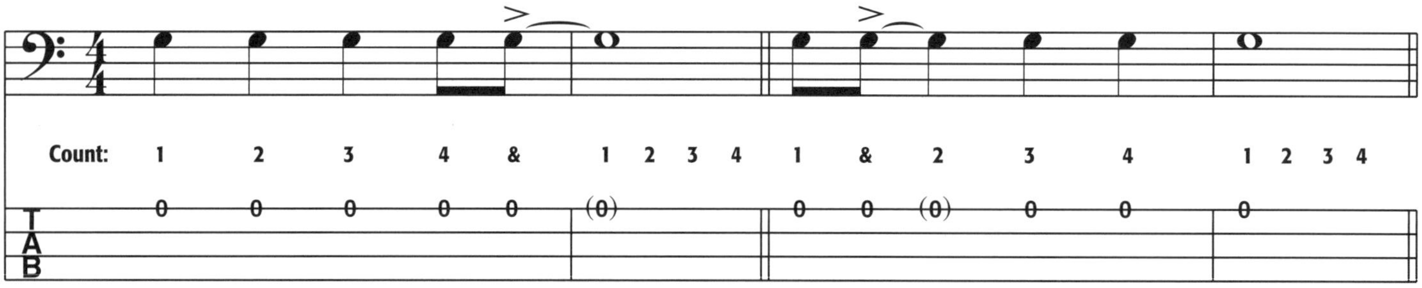

Example 5

Track 49

Beats 2 and 3 anticipated.

Example 6

Track 50

Beats 2, 3, and 4 anticipated.

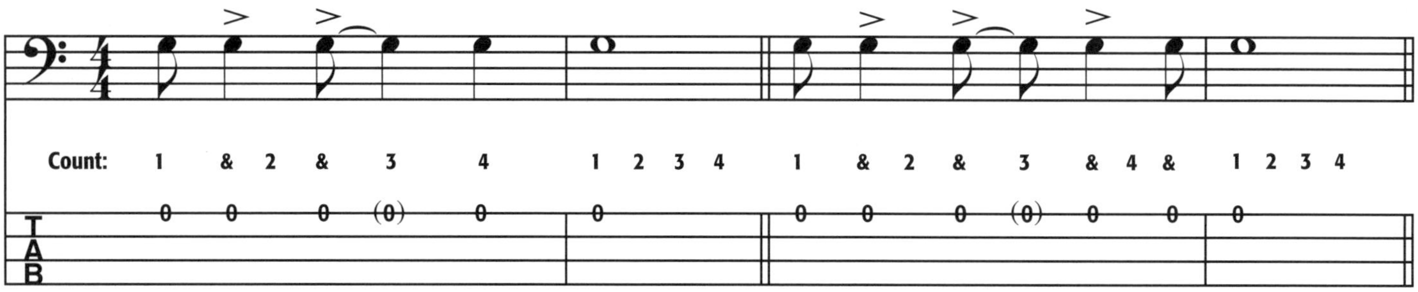

Syncopation in the Keys of C, G, F & B♭

Remember to count carefully and accent all the anticipated notes.

Syncopation Example in C

Track 51

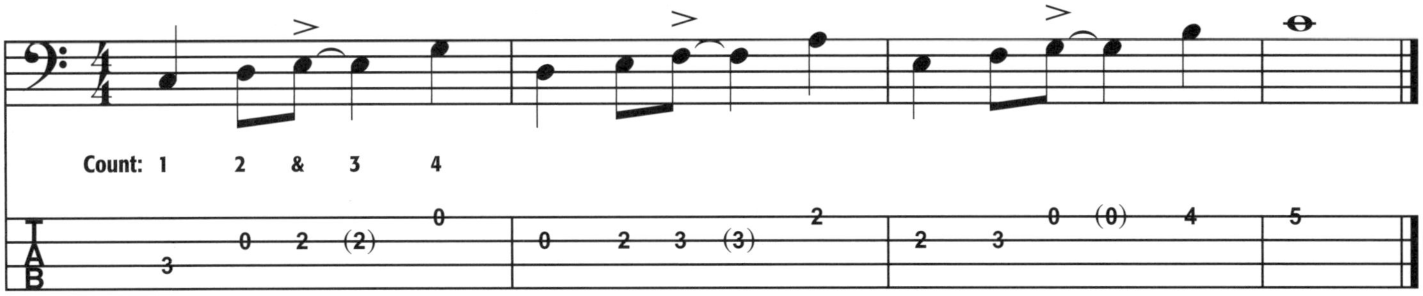

Syncopation Example in G

Track 52

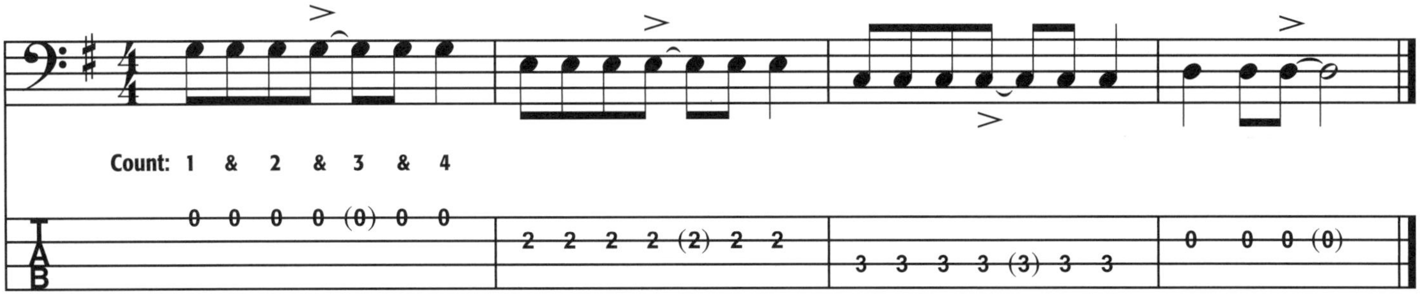

Syncopation Example in F

Track 53

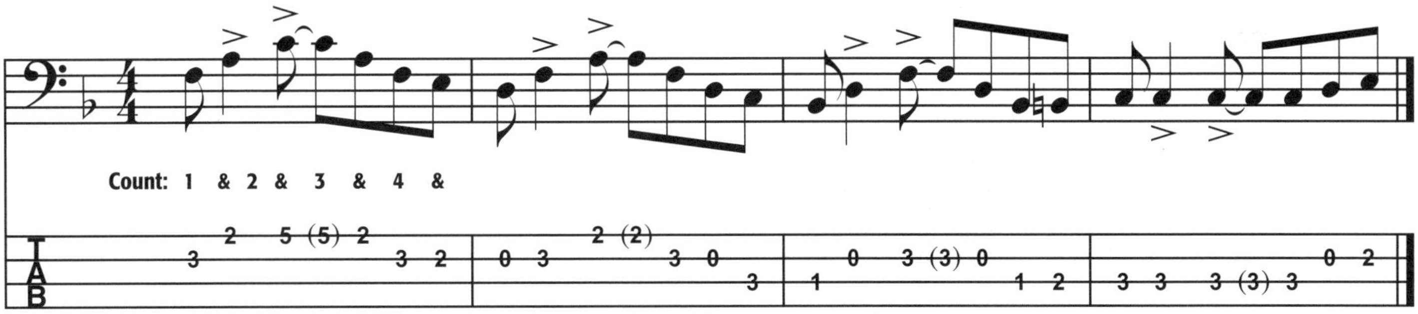

Syncopation Example in B♭

Track 54

3/4 Time & the Dotted Half Note

A New Kind of Note

Dotted Half Note

3 counts

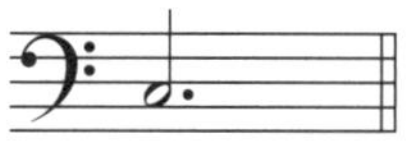

Count: 1 2 3

A New Time Signature

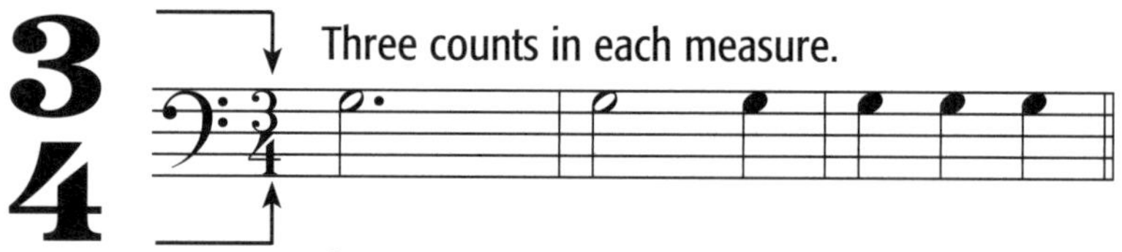

Playing Dotted Half Notes

Track 55

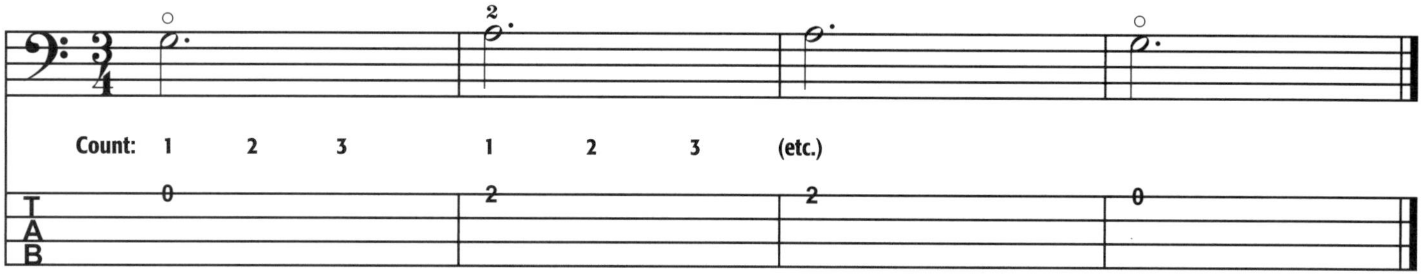

Photo © Ken Settle

Kim Gordon

Sonic Youth

Among those named by VH1 as the 100 Greatest Women of Rock is pioneer punk rock bassist Kim Gordon, whose abilities reach far beyond her part in the band Sonic Youth. After earning a degree in fine arts during the early 1970s, her creative endeavors went on to include solo recording, producing an album for Hole, and directing music videos for the Breeders. She also branched outside the musical arena, launching a line of clothing and modeling in ads for Calvin Klein.

Mixin' It Up in Three

Track 56

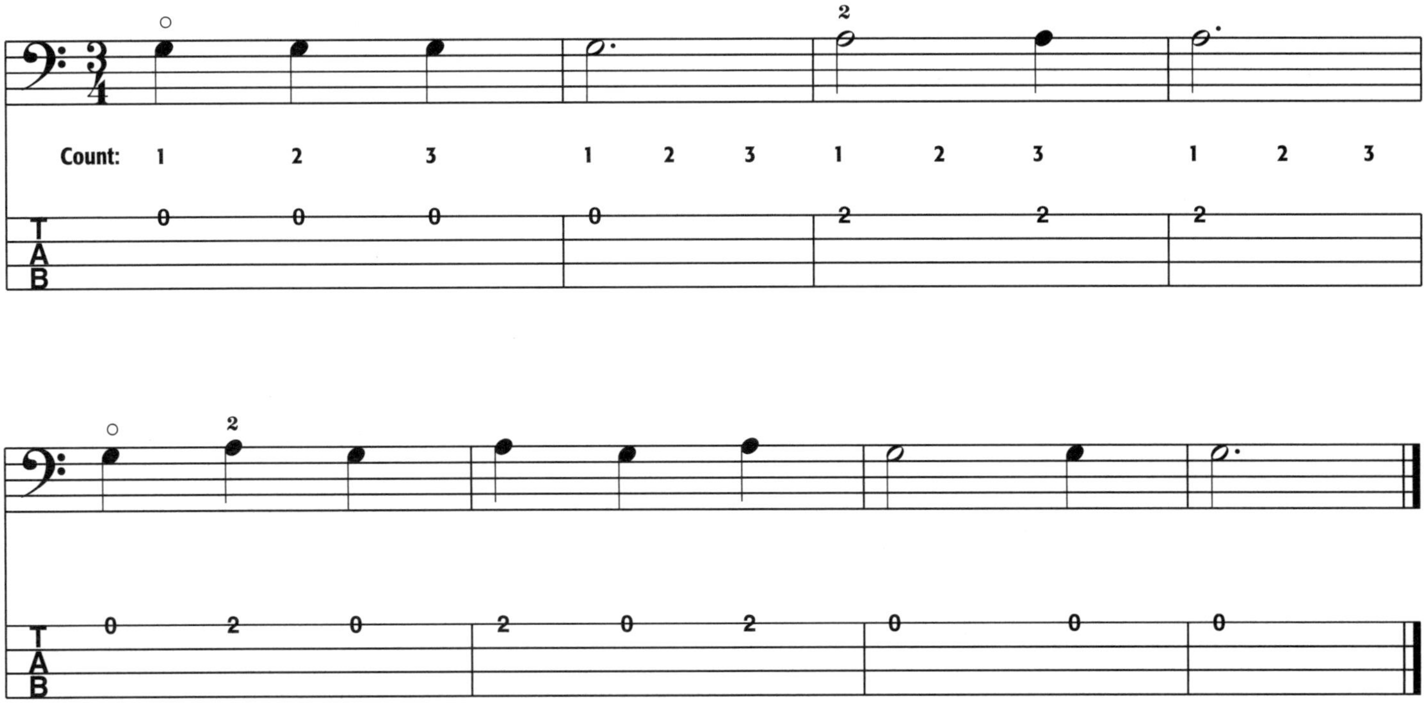

Extra Credit in Three

Track 57

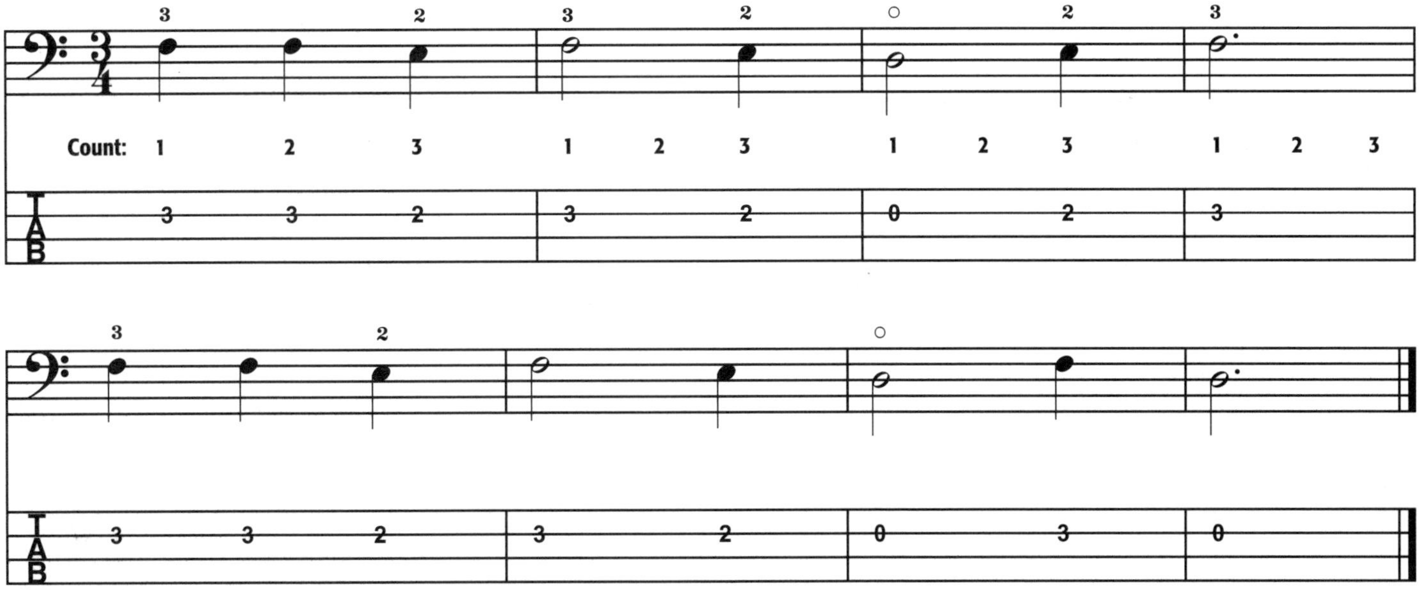

The Dotted Quarter Note

A dot to the right of a note increases its length by half. A dotted half note is equal to a half note tied to a quarter note for a total of three beats. A dotted quarter note equals a quarter note tied to an eighth note, which equals one and one-half beats.

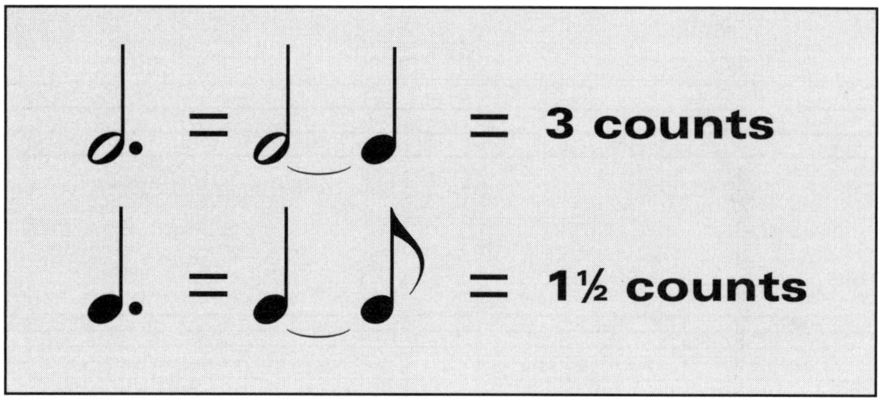

Preparatory Drill

Track 58

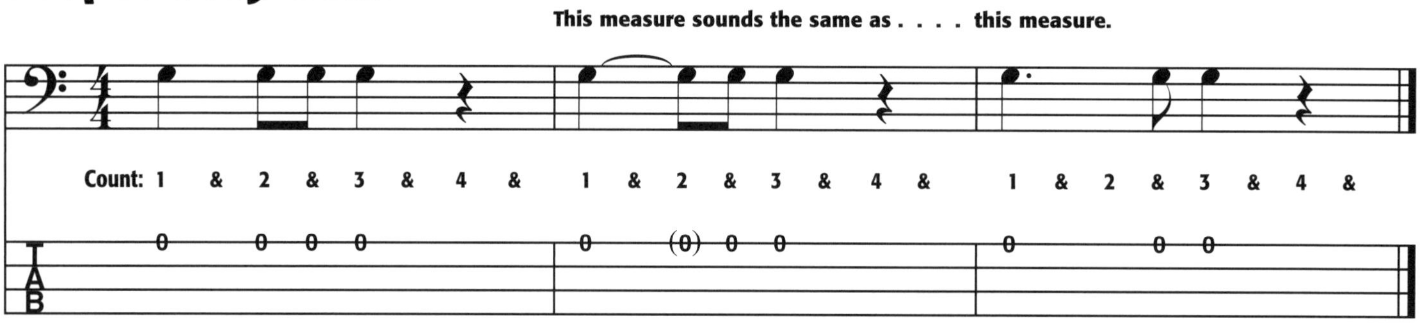

Go, Go, Go

Track 59

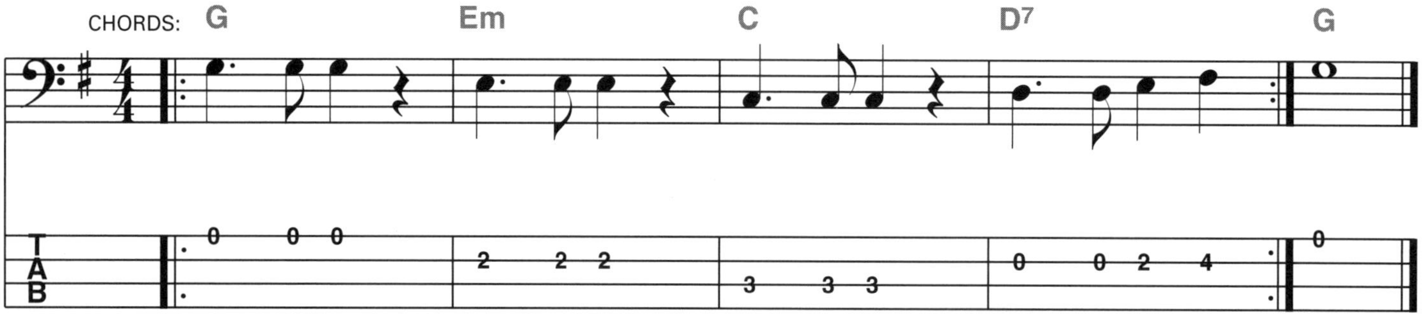

Combining Dotted Quarter Notes, Accents & Slides

Riff No. 1

Track 60

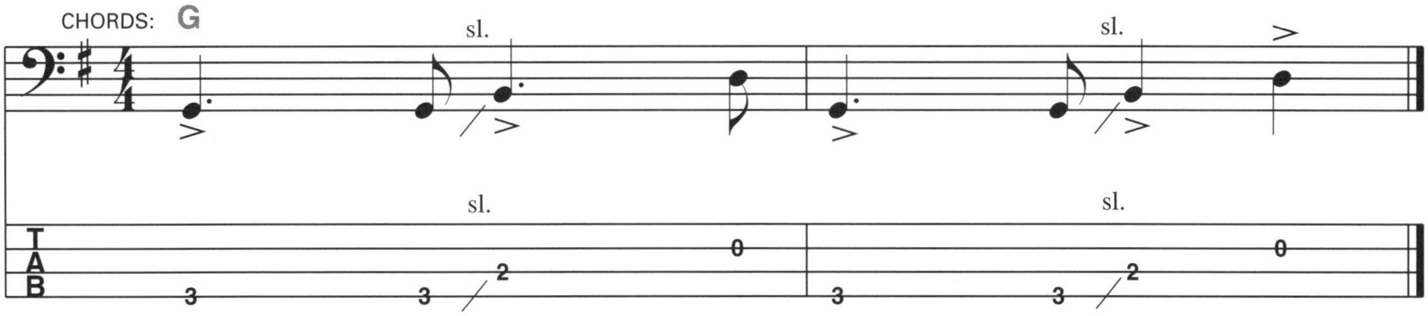

Riff No. 2

Track 61

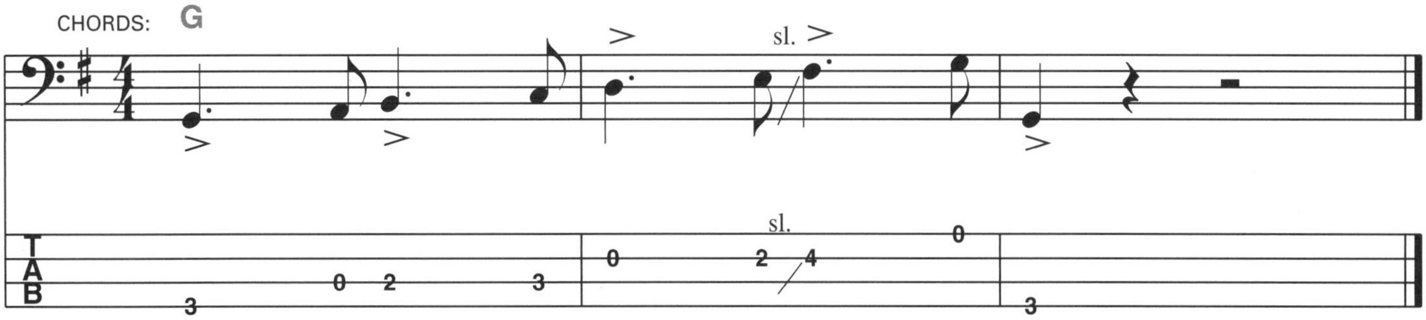

Rock Riffs with Syncopation

Rock Riff in C

Track 62

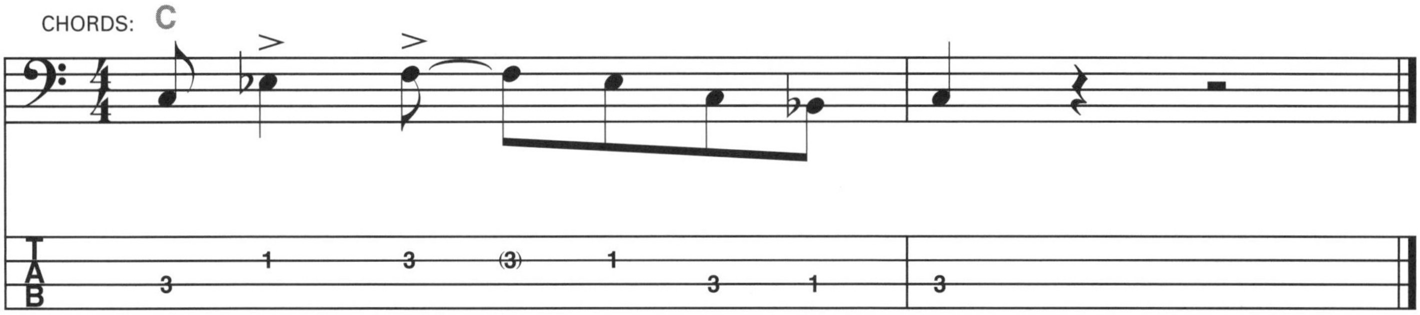

Rock Riff in F

Track 63

High C♯ (or D♭) & D

These notes further extend the upper range of notes you've learned so far. The fingering of these notes will vary depending upon the context of the music.

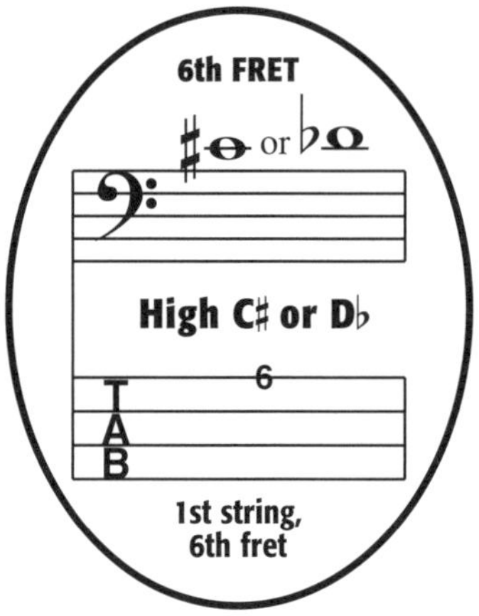

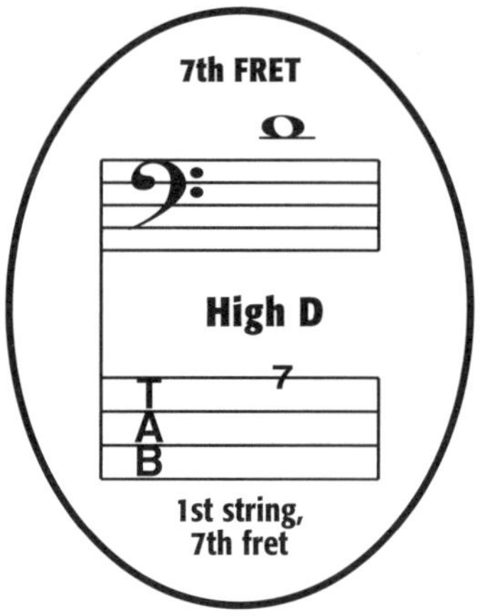

Exercise with High C♯ and D

Track 64

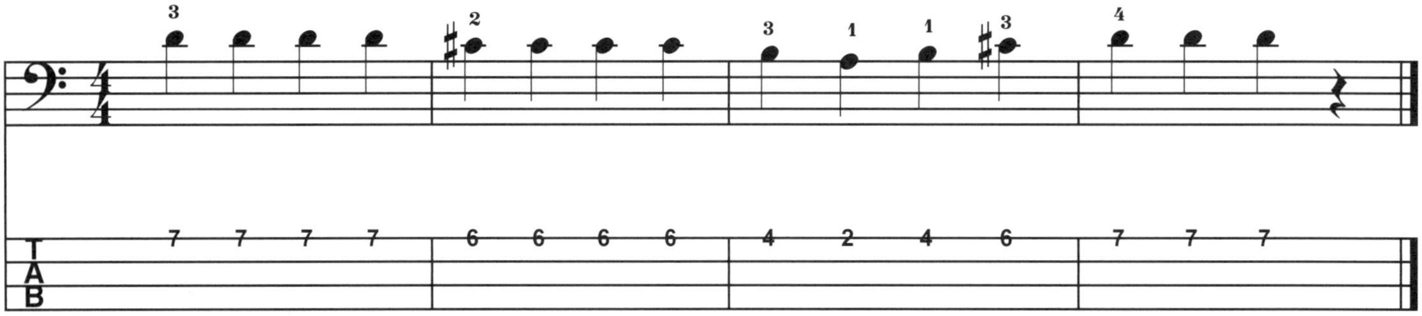

Exercise with High D♭

Track 65

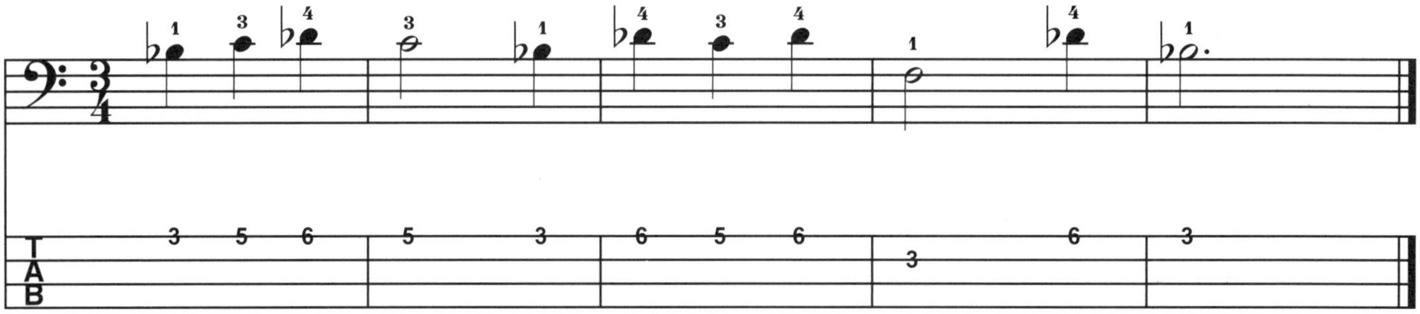

Michael Steele

The Bangles

When Sue Thomas changed her name to Micki Steele after being asked to join Joan Jett and Sandy West as the lead singer and bassist in an all-girl punk band called the Runaways, she had never played bass before. The producer who put the band together hired a teacher for her, and only five days after joining the band recorded a demo. Though her time with the Runaways lasted only four months and left her somewhat disillusioned, she would later change her name to Michael Steele and find worldwide success as the bassist for another all-girl band, the Bangles.

The Key of D Major

The key signature of two sharps (F♯ and C♯) tells you a piece is in the *key of D major*. All F's are played as F♯'s and all C's are played as C♯'s, unless preceded by a natural sign.

The D Major Scale

Track 66

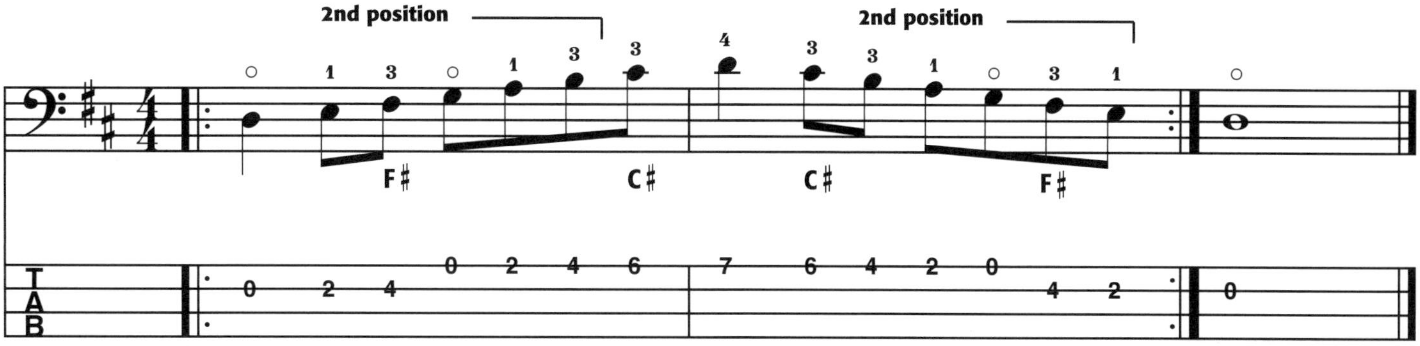

Joy to the World

Track 67

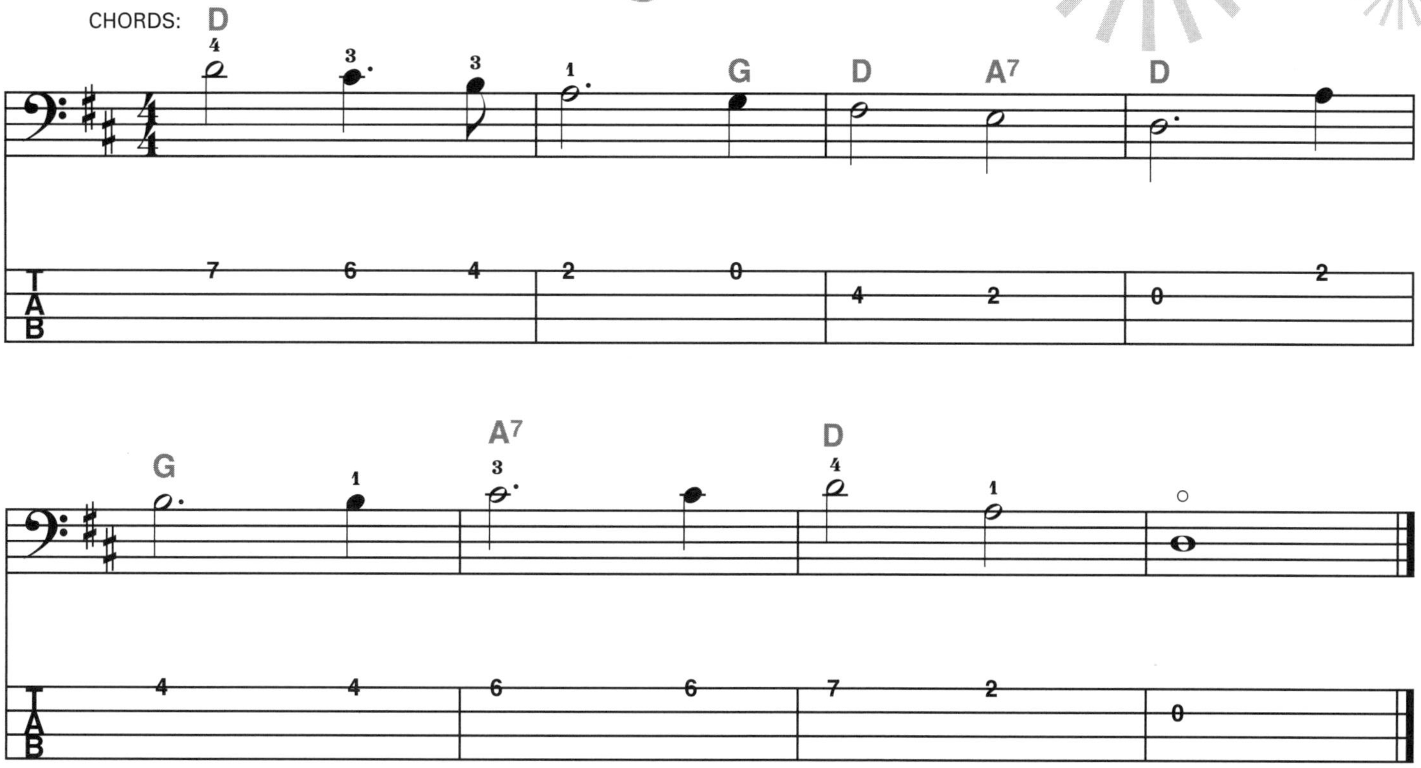

Sixteenth Notes & the Dotted 8th and 16th Note Rhythm

Sixteenth Notes

A sixteenth note is a black note with two flags added to the stem:

Two or more sixteenth notes are written with two beams connecting the stems:

Sixteenth notes are played four to a beat, twice as fast as eighth notes and four times as fast as quarter notes. In 4/4 time, there are four sixteenth notes per beat, and 16 sixteenth notes per measure.

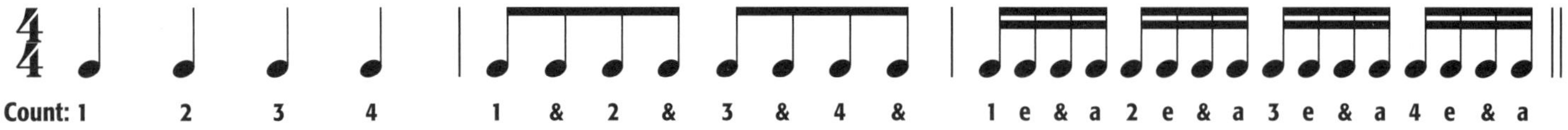

Dotted 8th and 16th Note Rhythm

The dotted 8th and 16th note rhythm is played in the time of one beat:

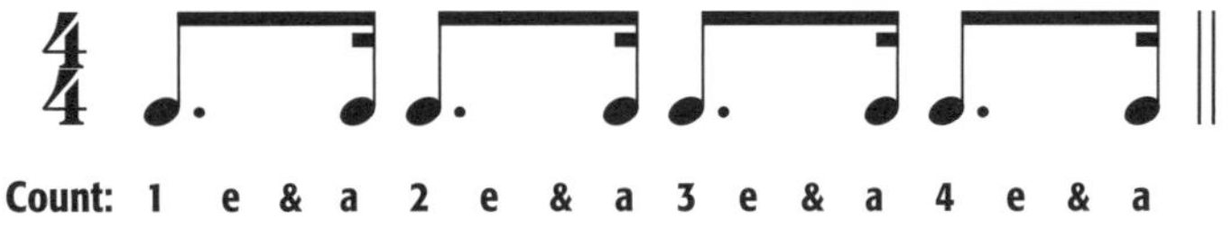

The dotted 8th and 16th note rhythm is used in many 1950s rock tunes and some blues. This rhythm is often called a *shuffle*. Practice the two examples below until you are comfortable with the feel.

Shuffle No. 1

Track 68

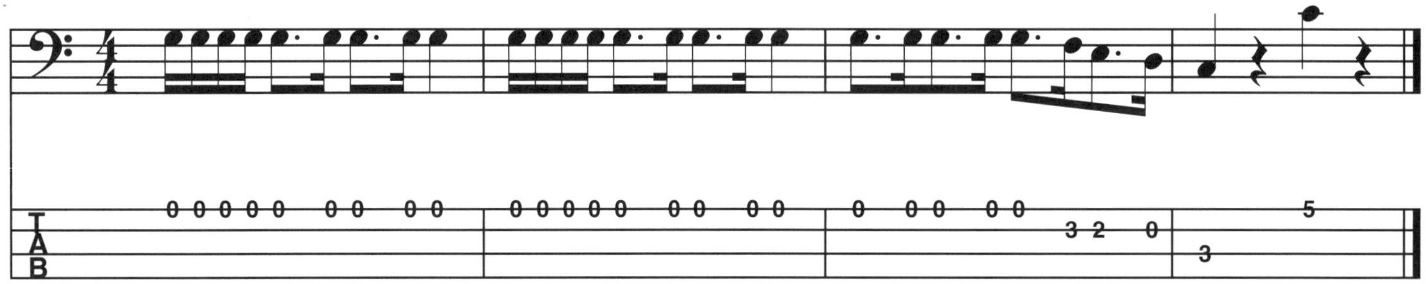

Shuffle No. 2

Track 69

The Key of A Major

A key signature of three sharps (F♯, C♯, and G♯) tells you a piece is in the *key of A major*. All F's are played as F♯'s, all C's are played as C♯'s, and all G's are played as G♯'s, unless preceded by a natural sign.

The key of A is very popular in rock and country music because it is an especially good-sounding key on the guitar.

The A Major Scale

Track 70

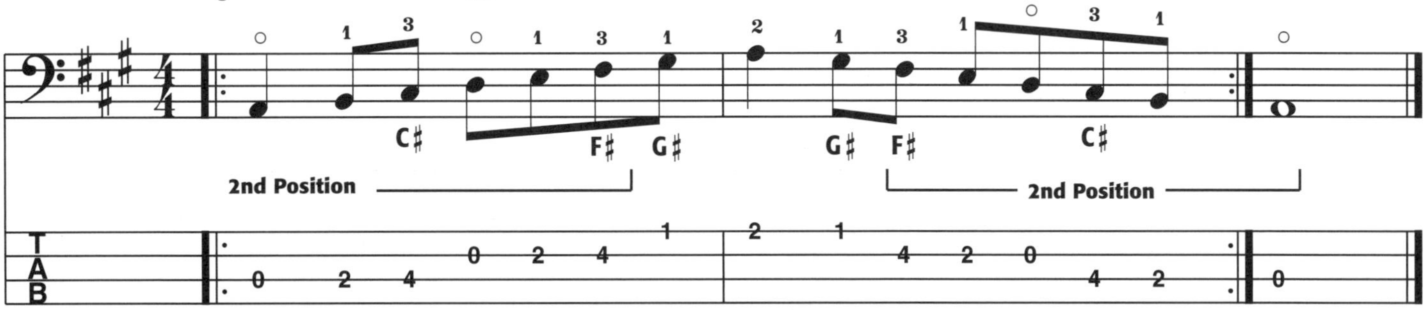

Incomplete Measures

Not every piece of music begins on beat 1. Music sometimes begins with an incomplete measure called a *pickup*. The beats in the pickup and the final bar of a piece will usually add up to one full measure: if the pickup is one beat, the last bar will have three beats in $\frac{4}{4}$ time or two beats in $\frac{3}{4}$ time.

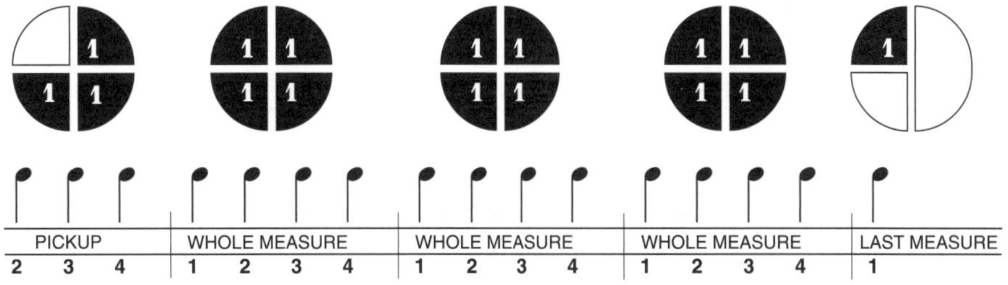

Mama Played Bass

Track 71

This example begins on beat 2 of the measure. The last measure has only one beat and combines with the three-beat pickup to make one complete bar of $\frac{4}{4}$ time.

D.C. stands for *da capo*, Italian words that literally mean "from the head." It tells you to repeat the music from the beginning.

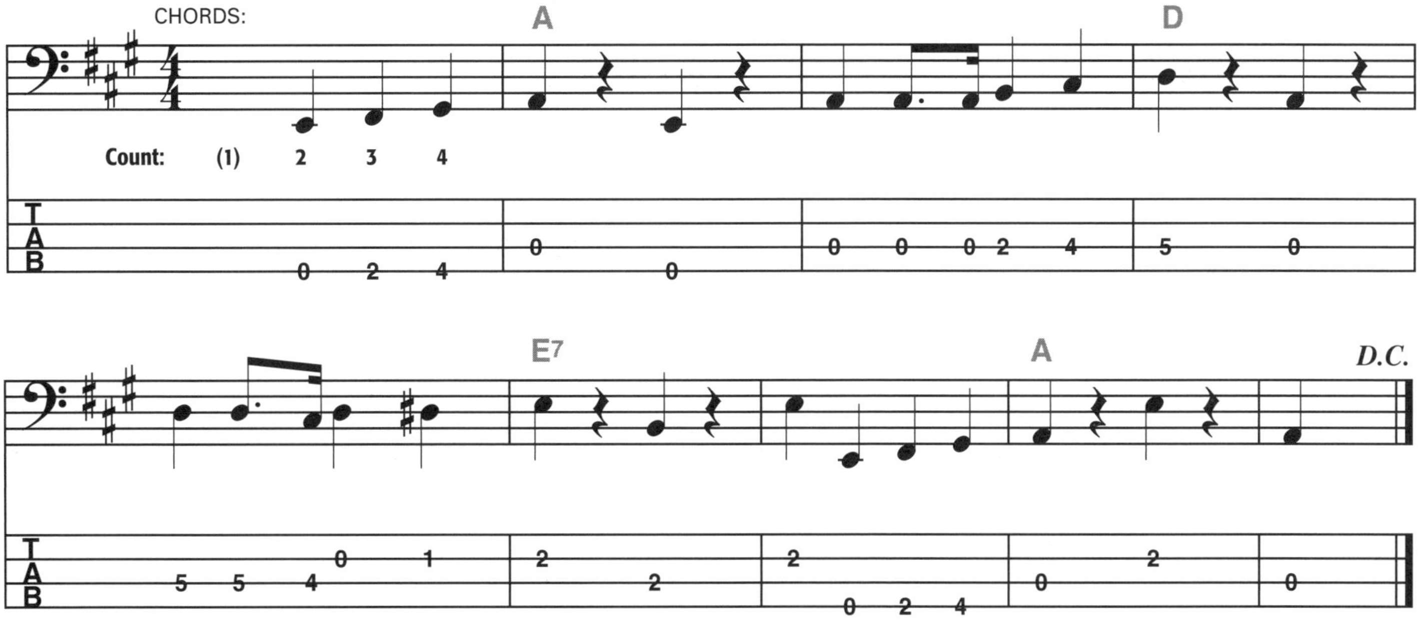

The Key of E Major

A key signature of four sharps (F♯, C♯, G♯ and D♯) tells you a piece is in the *key of E major.* All F's are played as F♯'s, C's are played as C♯'s, G's are played as G♯'s, and D's are played as D♯'s, unless preceded by a natural sign.

Like the key of A, the key of E is very important in rock, blues and country music because it sounds good on the guitar.

The E Major Scale

Track 72

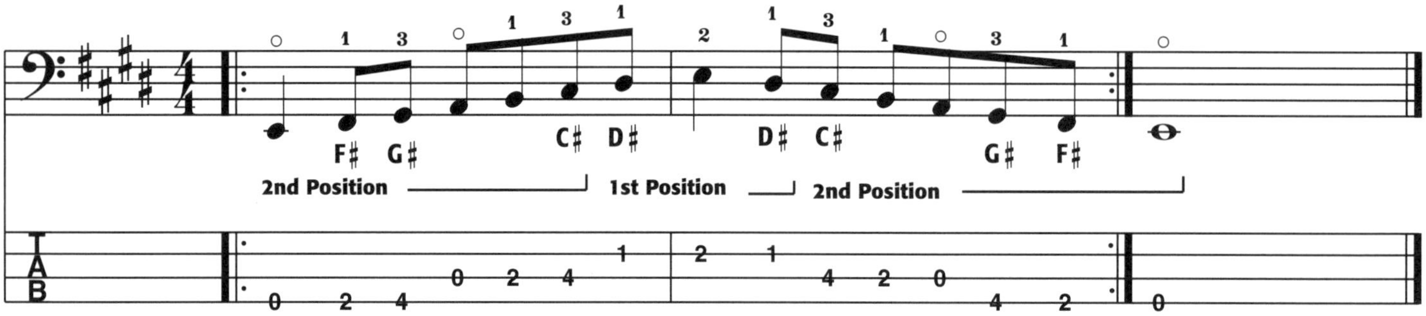

High D♯ (or E♭) & E

These notes will extend your upper register even further.

As with the notes learned on page 42, fingering depends on what precedes and what follows the note in question.

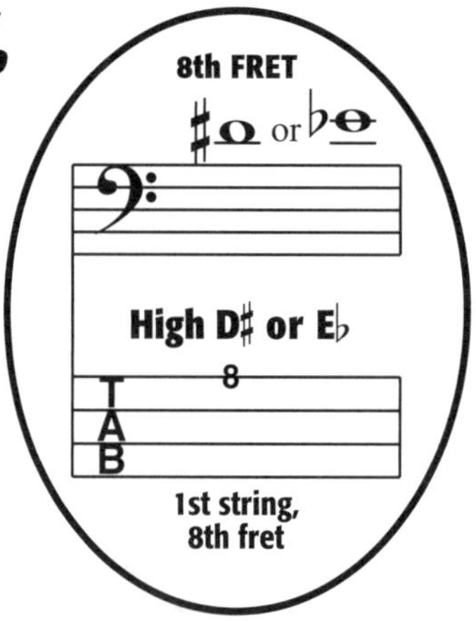

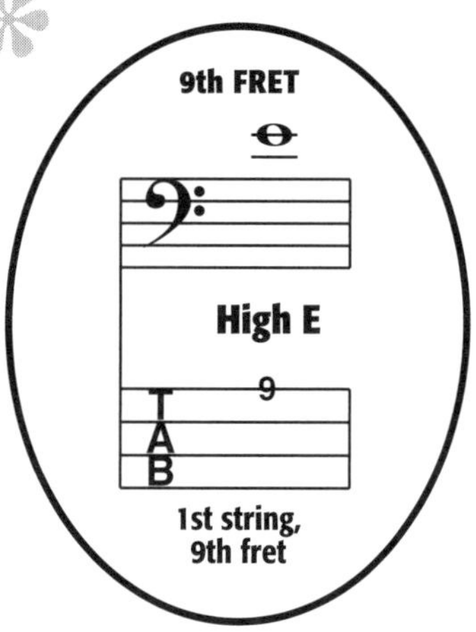

Exercise with High D♯ and E

Track 73

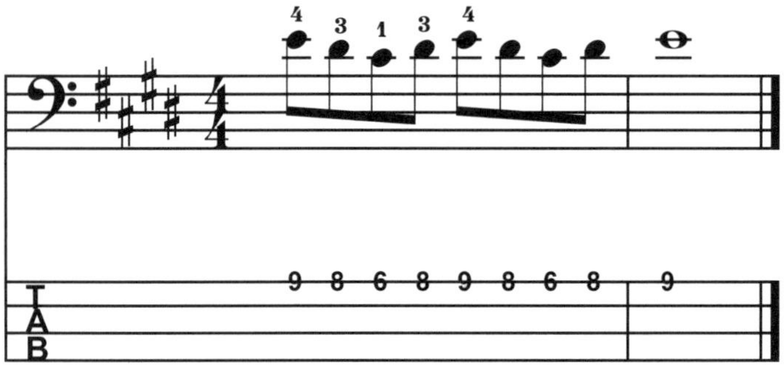

Exercise with High E♭

Track 74

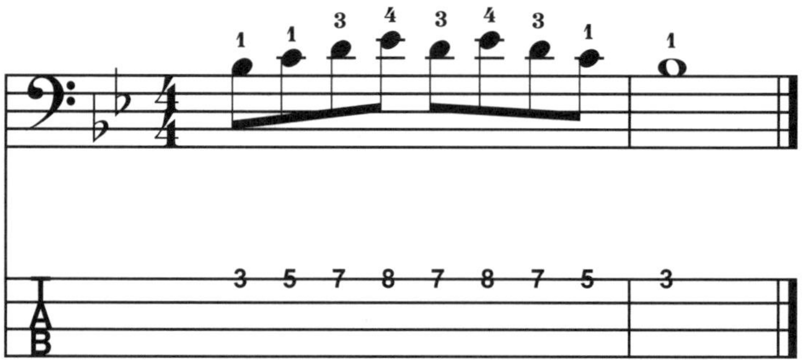

The Two-Octave E Major Scale

Track 75

Your knowledge of the notes high D♯ and E allows you to play an E major scale in two octaves. Add this scale to your daily practice.

Dreaming in E

Track 76

Bass Fingerboard Chart

The Bass Notes in the First Octave

The following chart shows the position of every bass note in the first octave (the first 12 frets). This includes every note used in this book as well as notes in the upper positions.

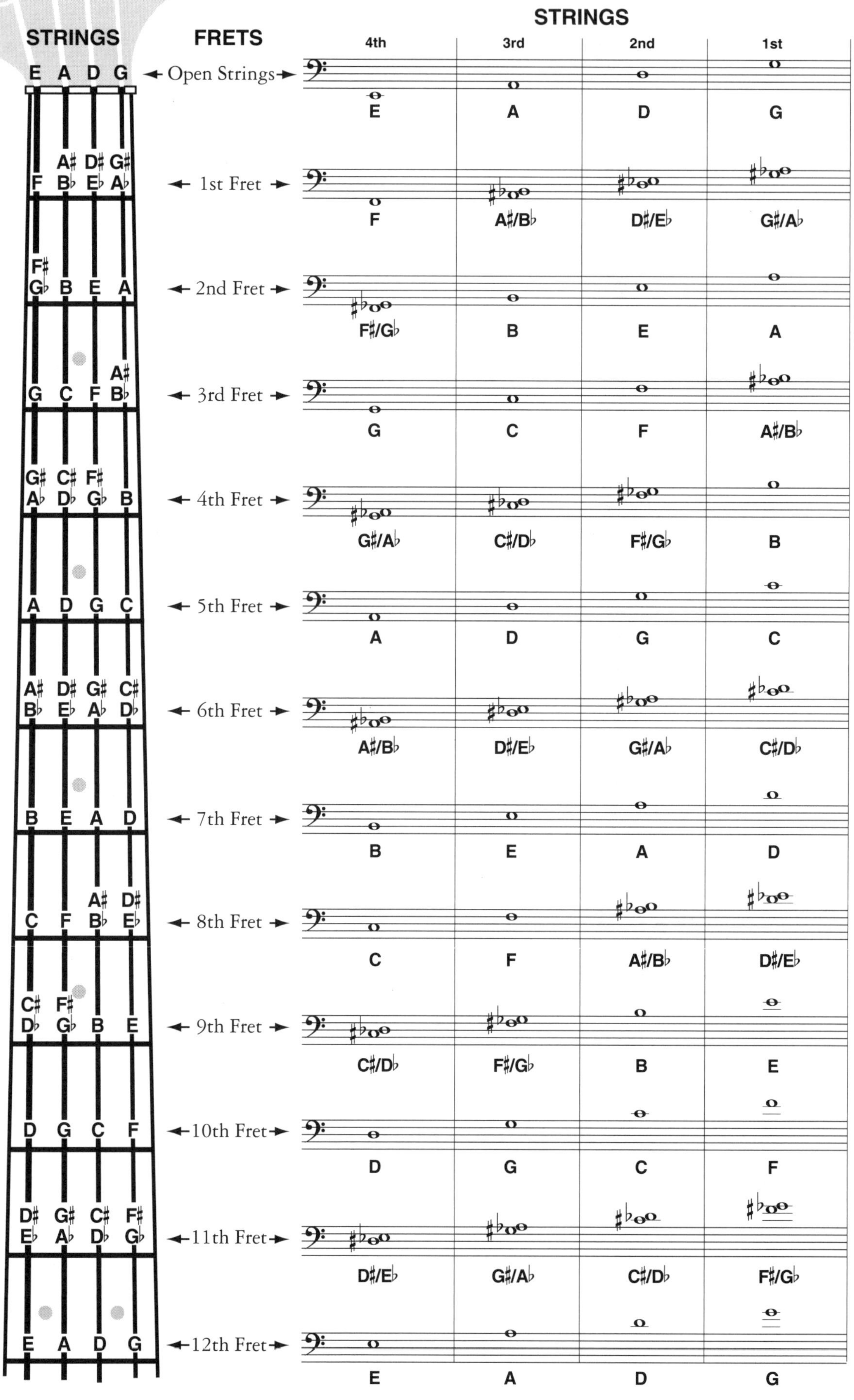